SPEAKING IN TONGUES AND PUBLIC WORSHIP

SPEAKING IN TONGUES AND PUBLIC WORSHIP

An Exegetical Commentary
on First Corinthians Fourteen

SPIROS ZODHIATES, TH.D.

AMG
PUBLISHERS
Chattanooga, TN 37422

Speaking in Tongues and Public Worship

An Exegetical Commentary
on First Corinthians Fourteen

Portions Taken From
Tongues?!
©1974, 1994 by Spiros Zodhiates

ISBN 0-89957-475-0

Printed in the United States of America
02 01 00 99 98 97 –R– 6 5 4 3 2 1

Contents

Preface

This book carefully examines 1 Corinthians 14 in detail from the Greek text. This chapter of the Word of God deals with two topics: speaking in tongues and women in the church. Some portions at the beginning of this volume originally appeared in my book entitled *Tongues?!*, which was written some twenty-five years ago.

There are three historical instances in the New Testament where people spoke instantly in languages that they had never learned. They were enabled to do so by the Holy Spirit. Furthermore, they were understood by those who heard them. These languages did not become permanent acquisitions of the speakers. They were not taught at a spiritual meeting. Is this the clear teaching of the Greek text? Did the Apostle Paul speak in tongues? Did he not say so in 1 Corinthians 14:18? "I thank my God, I speak with tongues more than ye all." What kind of utterance was he referring to? Was it the same as the historical instances in the Acts? Was it the same as the Corinthians used in their time of worship? Were these languages or ecstatic speeches? Is there one "unknown tongue," which is referred to in 1 Corinthians 13:1 as "the tongues of angels"? Could this be the same angelic language which would cause unbelieving listeners to say, "they are mad" ("maniacs," in the Greek text)—rather than to be attracted by it?

When I finished my book *Tongues?!* and sent a copy to my friend Dr. Heinz Horst Deichmann, an astute New Testament scholar, he scolded me for not including a study of the important, last eight verses of 1 Corinthians 14. At that time I considered myself inadequate to handle the task. Now I have been convicted that, although difficult, the role of women in the Christian church should not be ignored, but an attempt should be made to understand what Paul believed and wrote. Therefore, with fear and trembling, having finished sixteen volumes on 1 Corinthians, I come back to the unfinished task after having added much to my reservoir of knowledge of the New Testament: and so the last chapters of this book constitute a limited treatment of the role of women in the church.

This great apostle decided to stay single, because his avowed desire was to give his full attention to winning souls to Christ. He realized that a wife deserved attention second only to the Lord. However, being an apostle (1 Cor. 9:1, 2), he spoke authoritatively concerning both the single life and marriage. Of all the apostles, Paul wrote the most about the divine institution of marriage. He believed that he should not remain silent on the blessed role of a wife as revealed to him by the Lord. What Paul has to say, therefore, ought to be taken seriously by every Christian. "For this we say unto you by the word of the Lord" (1 Thess. 4:14). Although Paul had not experienced marriage himself, he was speaking by divine inspiration. We do well, therefore, to try to understand what he tells us regarding marriage and women, or wives, when it is in the Lord, which is the only way the Lord meant it to be.

Realizing that such an important role is given to wives for the maintenance of the family which is the foundation of society, we have decided to thoroughly examine why a bachelor such as Paul would write that "the wives [not women] in the churches should maintain silence" (1 Cor. 14:34; a.t.). Does God not want women to speak at all? And why should they keep silence "in the churches"? Maintenance of silence is a discipline, and as so many other traits of behavior, should be exercised under discipline.

Whether we like it or not, God designed women to be different than men. He further designed that women are to complement men, and within marriage to form a family, thus implementing the filling of the earth (Gen. 1:28). A man and a woman in marriage become one unit, one body, and they should have one head, otherwise disaster will result as each goes his or her own way. This is a mystery (Eph. 5:32). The church is also a mystery, and it is essential to understand the marriage relationship within the mystery of the church. Paul tells us how the control of the tongue contributes to the peace of both marriage and the church. We shall do well to listen to this great apostle as he writes under the inspiration of the Holy Spirit.

Hence, in this work on 1 Corinthians 14, we shall try to explain what Paul teaches on speaking in tongues and women in the church, with some reference to related verses outside of this chapter of the Scripture. This book is not, however, an exhaustive study of these topics; but study it carefully in anticipation of what Paul writes in his other epistles.

SPIROS ZODHIATES

An Overview of First Corinthians

Author: Paul the Apostle, author of thirteen other epistles to various individuals and congregations.

Date: About A.D. 55.

Recipients: The congregation which Paul established in Corinth.

Place: From Ephesus

Theme: Paul had received news about the Corinthian brethren from several sources (1 Cor. 1:11; 7:1; 16:17). The church was afflicted with many problems that face young churches and new converts. The Apostle, under the inspiration of the Holy Spirit, decided to write this urgent letter to admonish and instruct the church. Among other topics he discussed: the necessity of church discipline (5:1-13); divisions and disputes among Christians (1:10-16; 6:1-11); matters of conscience (8:1-13; 10:19-33); the support of preachers (9:1-27); abuses of the Lord's Supper (10:16-17, 21; 11:17-34); the misuse of spiritual gifts (12:1—14:40); and the importance of the resurrection of Jesus Christ (15:1-58).

An Outline of First Corinthians

In the days of the Apostle Paul, Corinth was the capital city of the Roman province of Achaia and the glory of Greece. Though its great ancient splendor had been destroyed by the Romans in 120 B.C., the city was rebuilt under Julius Caesar and restored to wealth and luxury under Augustus. Among all the cities of the world, however, it was most well known for its lewdness. The Apostle Paul lived in Corinth for eighteen months (Acts 18:11). After his departure, Paul went to Ephesus. During his three-year stay there, he heard reports of wickedness and division within the Corinthian church. In an effort to correct these evils, Paul wrote several letters to them, including the Epistle of First Corinthians.

1:1–9	The introductory remarks of Paul.
1:10–16	Paul condemns the divisions in the church and exhorts its members to unity.
1:17—2:16	Paul defends his ministry. He has preached the wisdom of Christ crucified. This wisdom is foolishness to the world, but is the glory of all those to whom the Spirit of God has revealed the truthfulness of it.
3:1–5	Paul declares that the simplicity of his teaching was due to the carnal state of the Corinthians, which state is clearly evidenced by their divisions.
3:6-23	Jesus Christ is the only foundation. Ministers are mere servants; the work is God's.
4:1–6	The duty of ministers is faithfulness.
4:6–21	Paul contrasts the arrogance and conceit of the false teachers to the humility and sacrifice of the apostles. Using his unique position as their spiritual father, Paul calls on the Corinthian believers to be discerning.

| **1 Cor. 14:1, 2** | *The Loving Way* |

Follow after charity, and desire spiritual gifts, but rather that ye may prophesy. For he that speaketh in an unknown tongue speaketh not unto men, but unto God: for no man understandeth him; howbeit in the spirit he speaketh mysteries.

Mysterious Tongues—What Good Are They?

If speaking in tongues were a real language taught and inspired by the Holy Spirit, then all who possessed this gift should be able to understand one another without the services of an interpreter. However such does not seem to have been the case in Corinth. We see no evidence of the creation of a totally new language that was useful in any respect. There were apparently as many "tongues" in Corinth as there were people who claimed to speak them. This is what caused so much confusion in the local assembly.

Let us examine the teaching of 1 Corinthians 14 regarding the practice of speaking with tongues in the Corinthian church. Verse 1 really belongs to chapter thirteen, in which Paul describes the characteristics of love, for it gives his concluding command, "Follow after charity, and desire spiritual gifts, but rather that ye may prophesy."

Follow after Charity

The word translated "follow after" is *diōkete* (1377) in Greek, which means "pursue, chase, hunt, run after," suggesting that love is elusive to the natural man. Love will not pursue us, as the devil does, but we must run after it, even as we are to seek God that we may find Him. The highest, the supreme, is not easily obtainable. This is the verb from which the noun *diōgmós* (1375), "persecution," comes. Circumstances of life often tend toward making love elude us. We must exercise conscious, active care never to lose sight of love—the kind of love Paul has just described in 1 Corinthians chapter thirteen. "Pursue the love," says Paul, "and desire spiritual ones" (literal translation). He does not say "gifts," but this is understood from the context. The special contrast here is between the gifts of prophesying and speaking with tongues. Love must come first in our lives before we begin talking about it. Let us never reverse the order.

Speaketh in an Unknown Tongue

In 1 Corinthians 14:2 Paul says, "For he that speaketh in an unknown tongue speaketh not unto men, but unto God: for no man understandeth him; howbeit in the spirit he speaketh mysteries." The word "unknown" in this verse does not occur in the Greek text. The translators inserted it to express their understanding of this phenomenon—a language unknown among men, not human, not understandable, a fabricated language that was not properly a language at all! Apparently it was a loud emotional outburst of sounds by which some thought they could communicate with God. Paul indicates in this verse that such a practice existed, but apparently only among the Corinthians, for it is never mentioned about other Christians or congregations. Paul's recognition of the existence of this unique practice among the Corinthians is not his approval of it. Instead his attitude seems to be, "We'll take you as you are and examine what you are doing." "With such unintelligible sounds you are evidently not speaking to men," he continues. It is useless to speak to men in a language you know they do not understand. "Therefore," Paul essentially says, "the only conclusion that you and I can come to about your practice is that you are speaking to God." Paul does not say that such utterances reach God or are God-ordained. Step by step he sets forth his argument in unimpeachable logic—for Paul was a master logician, as we see by his mighty arguments about the resurrection in chapter fifteen.

No One Understands This

"No one understands this babbling of yours," he tells them in 1 Corinthians 14:2. "Therefore, it is not a human language, it is not for men. If it is not for men, it must be for God." After all why should anyone want to communicate with God in a language unknown to him or to anyone else especially in public worship? Does God not understand all human languages? Does it make sense to speak to God without knowing yourself what you are saying? This is to do less than justice to His infinite majesty, greatness, and intelligence. Fundamentally prayer is the expression of our complete dependence and inadequacy. When we do not know what we are saying, we cannot express even that.

The Holy Spirit enabled people to speak with tongues at Pentecost, in the house of Cornelius at Caesarea, and in Ephesus so that others might hear and understand the message of God. Usefulness is a very important criterion of God's gifts. God does nothing, creates nothing, without a purpose. He gave us a brain, to think; He gives us food to nourish our bodies; He has provided salvation in Jesus Christ because we need it. Nothing is aimless or given for its sake, without regard to its purpose. Certainly this applies to the gift of speaking in tongues, providing a valuable criterion for whether such manifestations proceed from God or from our spirits. Since the basic purpose of speaking is to be understood, speaking to God or others in an unknown tongue cannot accomplish this. Moreover God communicates with us by speaking through His Word in language that we can understand. Let us then examine the argument by which we arrive at the conclusion that Paul uses the expression "speaking with tongues" here to refer to mere meaningless sounds.

But Rather That Ye May Prophesy

In 14:1 he says to the Corinthians, "Follow after charity [love], and desire spiritual gifts, but rather that ye may prophesy." The word "and" here is the correct translation of the Greek particle *dé* (1161). However, this particle is, to our way of thinking, incorrectly translated in the third clause of this verse. The way we translate this word often determines our understanding of the trend of thought. In chapter thirteen Paul has extolled love as the foremost and unifying spiritual gift. Now he begins chapter fourteen with the command. "Chase after love," followed by the clause, "and desire spiritual gifts" (a.t.). If the particle *dé* had been taken as an adversative and translated "but," it would place love in the category of nonspiritual gifts. "Having the basic substance of life, which is love," says Paul. "Seek in addition other lesser and particular spiritual gifts, the most important of which is prophesying."

"But rather that ye may prophesy" should really be "and rather [or moreover] that ye may prophesy," for it is the same word *dé* (1161) translated "and" in the second clause. There is no reason to take it as an adversative in this third clause. If we translated it "but rather that ye may prophesy," we would have to assume that "prophesying" is not a spiritual gift, which disagrees with the general teaching of Scripture and of Paul in particular. Prophesying, or speaking forth the oracles and commandments of God, is the product of love for God and men. It speaks a language that others understand. Its object is neither self nor God, but others to whom God wants to speak through us.

Others cannot understand this "tongue"; it is meant for God's ear only. Therefore it must consist of meaningless sounds. Certainly it stands in contrast to "prophesying," which because of its nature uses known, human, understandable languages. If it were comprehensible speech, Paul would have called it "prophesying." Paul goes on to give the reason a person who speaks in "a tongue" does not speak to men: "For no man understandeth him." "Understandeth" is *akoúei* (191) in the Greek, meaning "heareth." The "for" here would be more explicit if translated "indeed," or "in truth, in fact." "Indeed no one understands him"; therefore his language must be other than human, an ecstatic grouping of sounds, which only an omniscient God can understand.

In the Spirit He Speaketh Mysteries

The fourth clause of verse 2, "howbeit in the spirit he speaketh mysteries," again uses the particle *dé* (1161). Is this a connective or an adversative? It would seem to us that the "howbeit" of the KJV might better be expressed by the translation "indeed, in fact," as the argument here couples with the previous one. "No one understands incoherent sounds," runs the argument, "and therefore he is speaking mysteries in the spirit." The word "spirit" does not refer to the Holy Spirit here, but to the spirit of the one speaking. Verse 14 makes this indisputable since it uses the possessive pronoun "my" (*mou*) and the definite article "the" (*tó*, 3588). "For if I pray in an unknown tongue, my spirit prayeth, but my understanding is unfruitful." The literal Greek is "the spirit mine." One never finds the Holy Spirit speaking words that cannot be understood. The Holy Spirit reveals the mind and purpose of God and never conceals them. What would be the use of speaking to men in languages they could not understand?

Verse 16 also makes it clear that the word "spirit" refers to the speaker's spirit and not God's. It states "Else, when thou shalt bless with the spirit." How can you or I bless with the Spirit of God? We are not the ones who administer His Spirit. Moreover how is it possible to bless someone with the Holy Spirit (if this were conceivably the Holy Spirit) and to have the person be blessed and say "Amen," if he does not understand you? The subject of this whole sentence is the person who speaks in a tongue that no one can understand, and who is therefore speaking in his spirit things that are mysteries to himself, creations of his imagination. The word *pneúmati* (4152), "by spirit," is further evidence that it is not the Spirit of God speaking through him to others, as happened at Pentecost, but his spirit expressing itself unintelligibly. The Corinthian ecstatic utterances were the creation of their spirits.

One great difficulty of the Christian life is to recognize which of our activities and utterances are the product of the Holy Spirit and which are of our spirits. Since Paul says that these tongues were not known, human languages, that they were not prophesying, that they were directed to God only, that they were the product of man's spirit, and that nobody could understand them, we must conclude that Paul condemns them as meaningless.

<u>LESSONS</u>:

1. The first verse of 1 Corinthians 14 should be associated directly with the preceding chapter about love (1 Cor. 13).
2. Love must be diligently sought after; it does not come easily to the natural man.

THE LOVING WAY

3. The word "unknown" is not in the Greek text. The translators of the King James Version inserted it, putting it in italics. They believed this phenomenon was an unknown, incomprehensible, fabricated non-language.

4. The Apostle Paul did not approve of the practice of spontaneous, loud, emotional outbursts of sounds which some Corinthians believed to be valid communications to God. There is no evidence that glossolalia occurred in any other congregation in the New Testament. Why? Because the Corinthians were spiritually the least mature.

5. Why speak to people in a language you know they do not understand? If you say, "It is not for men" then you must be directing it toward God. If that is the case, since God already understands all human languages, why would you want to address God and not know yourself what you are saying? Besides all this, babbling ecstatically creates much confusion in the congregation and among the visitors.

6. Unprofitable tongue-speaking is sharply contrasted with profitable prophesying which used known, understandable, human languages.

7. Members of the Corinthian congregation were creating the occurrences of these ecstatic utterances by their spirits, not the Holy Spirit. Paul says that these utterances were without meaning.

1 Cor. 14:3, 4 | *Our Speech Must Be Helpful to Others*

But he that prophesieth speaketh unto men to edification, and exhortation, and comfort. He that speaketh in an unknown tongue edifieth himself; but he that prophesieth edifieth the church.

But He That Prophesieth

"But he that prophesieth," says Paul, "speaketh unto men to edification, and exhortation, and comfort" (1 Cor. 14:3). This verse presents the contrast between the unintelligible utterances of the previous verse and the prophesying which Paul commends. The two verses are not connected but stand in opposition to each other. The one who speaks "a tongue" cannot be understood by anyone but God. What he says is mysterious, the product of his spirit and imagination. When Paul speaks of "interpretation" accompanying "tongues," he refers to a language that the interpreter can understand. If it cannot be understood, it cannot be interpreted; any attempt at interpretation would be mere conjecture. One can only interpret knowable languages.

The claim by some that the tongues of 1 Corinthians chapter fourteen are angelic languages that only the Spirit of God can interpret and thus make understandable seems untenable for the following reasons:

If this were so, Paul would commend speaking with those angelic heavenly tongues.

Whenever God or angels speak to men in Scripture, they do so in human languages so that they can be understood. If this is God's method, why should it be otherwise with God's children? His methods and practices should be ours as well. If God did not employ an unknown, heavenly, angelic language to speak to us, why should we find it either necessary or desirable to do so when speaking to Him or to our fellowmen? His message must be understood if it is to be heeded, and so must ours.

Since interpretation seems to be a prerequisite to speaking in an unknown tongue, it must be that the meaning of what is said is the important thing, rather than the speaking itself. Why, then, should God speak to us in a language we cannot understand, since understanding is His purpose? His message is always direct and understandable, and ours should be also.

In contrast to this non-interpretable, unknowable utterance stands prophesying. "But he who prophesies speaks to men . . ." (1 Cor. 14:3). Prophecy is knowable, understandable human language. Paul uses the term in its widest sense as speaking forth of the Word of God and in its narrower sense as revealing the future. Who are prophets in this sense? Not only those specially designated as such in the Old Testament, not only ordained ministers, but all believers. All true Christians are to be prophets of God for the edification, exhortation, and comfort of other believers and of unbelievers. Let us refrain from placing unnecessary, non-existent distinctions between clergy and lay people, remembering that the Lord hath made all who believe "kings and priests unto God and his Father" (Rev. 1:6).

God gave mankind speech as a tool to communicate with his fellowman. Strictly speaking, in communicating with God speech is not necessary except in public worship, where it is primarily for the worshipers to know what is being said. Being understood is a first and necessary step to edification, exhortation, and comfort. Our speech must always have a purpose. We must always ask ourselves, "Does anyone but me benefit from what I am saying?" If not, says Paul, love requires that you keep quiet. Paul does not refer to personal edification in this verse, but speaking for the benefit of others; the whole context here is the local assembly of believers.

The person speaking must not only make himself understood, but must understand for himself what he is doing; he must consciously seek to edify others. More important than what we say is why we say it. This "why" must be consciously unselfish; love must motivate our prophesying. Prophesying not only contrasts with speaking in tongues, but can also be called its exact opposite. When you produce unintelligible sounds, you do not know what you are saying, and neither does anyone else. If this were of God, then it should edify others, and you would do it out of a conscious desire to edify. This desire to edify is a good criterion for all our speech.

Edification

The word for edification is *oikodomēn* (3619), from *oíkos* (3624) meaning "a home" and *demō* meaning "to build." When we prophesy we must build others spiritually. Paul makes this positive statement about prophecy to imply its negative about the selfish aspect of speaking with unknown tongues. The lack of prophecy in speaking with tongues can only tear down the spiritual house of God; it never builds. A builder knows what he is doing, and others see that his efforts make sense. He does not throw bricks and mortar together haphazardly, hoping that something worthwhile will result, but he systematically lays the bricks one on top of the other according to recognized construction principles. Likewise the content of prophecy must be inherently edifying.

This edification applies not only to believers but also to unbelievers. When applied to believers, it refers to their spiritual growth; when applied to unbelievers, to their addition to the body of Christ. The purpose of prophesying must be to build up individuals in the most holy faith, as well as to build up the holy faith itself through numbers. Prophecy accomplishes what speaking with tongues does not. Paul seeks to clarify for the Corinthians this sharp contrast between the unselfishness of the one and the self-centeredness of the other.

Exhortation

In the body of Christ, we need to encourage one another in spiritual matters, which is why Paul gives as the second purpose of our speaking *paráklēsin* (3874), "exhortation," or "encouragement." This is a distinctive feature of the proclamation of the gospel—exhorting men to come to Christ for salvation. There is no encouragement greater than to have one's sins forgiven. It uplifts all of life. Yet how can speaking in tongues encourage or exhort those in need of spiritual uplift?

Comfort

The third purpose of prophesying is *paramuthía* (3889), "comfort." This Greek noun occurs nowhere else in the New Testament. It has special reference to the consolation the Christian needs in view of the world's hostility. The teaching of God's Word, presented understandably, can comfort him in persecution and affliction; one cannot say the same of unintelligible utterances. They provide no real comfort to the speaker or the hearer; but he who speaks a word of comfort to a brother unwittingly comforts himself in the process.

Edifieth Himself

In the very next verse, Paul reverts to the subject of speaking in a tongue, that is, incoherent utterance. Referring to some individual among the Corinthians, he says, "He that speaketh in an unknown tongue edifieth himself" (1 Cor. 14:4). Although the word "unknown" is not in the Greek text, its use is justified because it so aptly describes this phenomenon. To have an ecstatic emotional experience may have some value in making you feel closer to God. Paul does not deny this. Emotionalism uplifts and edifies many people who find this to be the best way they can know God, among them are the Corinthians. But this peculiar ecstatic experience of theirs was never ascribed to the Philippians, the Ephesians, the Thessalonians, or any other group of Christians whom Paul knew. This practice, says Paul, constitutes a selfish enjoyment of religious experience, "edifieth himself." He does not say that this is commendable; here he merely states a fact—that there is some edification in it, but that it is exclusively for self. If others were able to understand it, they, too, might be edified; but since they are not edified, it is obvious that it is mere meaningless sound.

The Church

No definite article precedes the word *ekklēsían* (1577), "church," here, so that it refers to any local assembly of believers. Who is the troublemaker in the local assembly? He who believes that the interest of God and others should center in himself. A self-centered person who seeks to appropriate all God's blessings for his benefit, even if those benefits are spiritual, causes division and trouble in the local congregation. Also such a person, says Paul, is the one who speaks in an incomprehensible tongue, to build up himself.

Too often "speaking in tongues" becomes a matter of public ostentation, with no possible edifying effect on those who hear it. Furthermore it has the rather unfortunate effect of causing others, especially unbelievers, to feel that Christians are mentally unbalanced.

LESSONS:

1. Allegedly no one except God could understand the person "speaking in a tongue." The talk was mysterious since the utterances originated from the person's spirit and imagination.
2. Since one could only interpret knowable languages, the "interpretation" of this incomprehensible glossolalia was impossible. The meaning held importance, not the speaking itself.
3. No record exists of an angel ever speaking to human beings in an incomprehensive language.
4. Knowable, understandable "prophesying" was the presentation of the Word to benefit all the hearers.
5. Although some esoteric, mystical value might accompany an ecstatic emotional experience, here the Apostle Paul was saying that it was selfish enjoyment of a religious experience which excluded the local assembly of believers. In truth, not only was it unedifying to Christian bystanders, it might have caused unbelievers to think that some were mentally unbalanced.

1 Cor. 14:5

The Gift of Languages

I would that ye all spake with tongues, but rather that ye prophesied: for greater is he that prophesieth than he that speaketh with tongues, except he interpret, that the church may receive edifying.

I Would That Ye All Spake with Tongues

After Paul extols "prophesying" as opposed to "speaking with tongues," he goes on to say, "I would that ye all spake with tongues, but rather that ye prophesied" (1 Cor. 14:5). At first glance, this might be a bit mystifying, since Paul did not commend the Corinthian practice of tongue-speaking, and tried to curtail its manifestations. Moreover observe that the translators did not translate this "unknown tongues," as in verse 2, but "tongues," for they realized that this expression could not mean ecstatic, unintelligible sounds. This chapter uses the plural form of the word here, referring to the ability to speak in languages other than one's own to tell the wonders of God. Nevertheless, he says, before you attempt to witness in foreign languages, first speak in your own. It is all too human to wish we could preach in foreign countries while doing nothing about witnessing to our people in our language. Use what you know, admonishes Paul. How we need to heed his advice! Note carefully the following:

Ye All

The word *pántas* (3956), "all," in this verse does not mean all believers in general, nor all the believers in Corinth to whom Paul was writing as a group. It has rather the meaning of *hékastos* (1538), "each one within a group" (see Liddell and Scott, *Greek-English Lexicon.* Oxford: Clarendon Press, 1958, p. 1345). Paul knew that not all the Corinthian Christians were able to speak in unknown tongues (languages), so why should he wish something especially for them that he never wished for the most spiritual group of believers, the Philippian church, for instance. If these ecstatic utterances (if that is the meaning of the word "tongues" in 1 Cor. 14:5) were something really to be desired, and so very essential a manifestation of the Holy Spirit's presence, then Paul would have expressed a wish that all Christians everywhere might share in this experience. But he did not do so.

It is quite probable that all the people in Corinth knew at least two languages, the one native to them and the one native to Corinth. I lived in Egypt for twelve years, during which time I associated with non-Arabic-speaking people; but all of us—Greeks, Armenians, Frenchmen, Americans, and other foreigners—usually spoke our own particular native language and also Arabic, the language of the land. The same thing is true in America among the foreigners dwelling within its borders. In Corinth, the foreigners must have spoken in their own native languages and also in Greek, the language of Corinth. This is highly desirable and useful, and when consecrated to God's service can make His Word widely known.

Spake with Tongues

It is with this background that Paul says, "I wish that every one of you spoke with languages other than your own because this would enable you to prophesy in more than your own native tongue" (a.t.). Notice again that we say, with good reason, that the term "tongues" means foreign languages here and not an unknown ecstatic lingual utterance. We must purge ourselves of the notion that the word "tongues" in 1 Corinthians 12—14 always means unknown or ecstatic lingual utterance because if it does, much of what Paul says makes no sense whatever. To be a linguist is not sufficient, however because you can use your skill for purely self-serving purposes, such as getting along in business. That was not the reason Paul wanted these Christians to speak various languages. "I would . . . rather that ye prophesied," not merely spoke in foreign languages but prophesied in them. This is the same principle he set forth in 1 Corinthians 10:31, when he said, "Whether therefore ye eat, or drink, or whatsoever ye do, do all to the glory of God." Whatever we are or do must bear testimony to the saving grace of the Lord Jesus Christ, that in all things He might have the preeminence. All our human capabilities must serve the divine purpose.

Paul goes from the simple infinitive construction *lalein* (2980) *glōssais* (1100), "to speak in languages," which expresses the mere wish that these Corinthians could do so, to the more intense and climactic *hína* (2443), "in order that," giving strong purpose to his wish, and in this context coupling it with the adverb *mállon* (3123), "more so," or "more strongly." The particle *dé* (1161), translated "but," is a correlative conjunction here rather than an adversative one, and should therefore be translated as "and" or "moreover." Paul is not contrasting the speaking in foreign languages (so naturally desirable for each of the believers in Corinth) with prophesying or witnessing, but is bringing out that the one makes the other more fully possible. To paraphrase it accurately "I wish each one of you spoke in other languages; and it is even more wonderful to use this gift or talent to prophesy." The fulfillment of the divine purpose completes the purpose of the natural gift.

I Would That

The emphasis of the verb *thélō* (2309) "I wish," applies more to the second clause of verse 5 than to the first. Freely translated it would read, "And I wish that each [all] of you would speak foreign languages, and still more that ye may prophesy." "Still more that ye may prophesy" is his paramount wish, which, however, is the complement of the basic presupposition that they are able to speak in a variety of human languages. Nowhere else does the Apostle Paul use the expression *thélō* . . . *hína* (2443), "I wish . . . that ye may." The object of the wish is indicated by the clause introduced by *hína*, "that ye may prophesy." His wish was more concerned with the prophesying than with the speaking in foreign languages. His stress is on the purpose of language and not on the mere ability to speak more than one language. It is good to have abilities, whether naturally or supernaturally acquired, but their real value lies in the use we make of them. Prophesying makes the knowledge of languages useful, serviceable, beneficial.

Greater Is He

The second part of this verse states the principle, "For [in fact] greater is he that prophesieth than he that speaketh with tongues, except he interpret, that the church may receive edifying." The particle *dé* (1161) here, translated "for," has more the strength of "in fact, now, indeed, really." the clause being an emphatic explanation and a conclusion of what the Apostle has just finished saying. "Really," says Paul, "greater is he that prophesieth than he that speaketh with tongues." The word *meízōn* (3187), "greater," is used repeatedly by Paul in his letters to the Corinthians. Greatness was their ambition, the aspiration of selfishness.

And this greatness they mistakenly sought in "unknown tongues," thinking that this was the same manifestation of the Holy Spirit demonstrated at Jerusalem, Caesarea, and Ephesus.

But even if these had been human languages, prophesying would still be greater than tongues, says Paul. Just to be able to speak in languages is of no value in God's sight; only if our linguistic ability is used for the glory of God in prophesying does it acquire value. This holds good with all kinds of knowledge; indeed it is the basis of the Apostle's argument throughout the thirteenth chapter of 1 Corinthians. "Though I speak with the tongues of men and of angels," Paul says, "and have not charity [love], I am become as sounding brass, or a tinkling cymbal. And though I have the gift of prophecy, and understand all mysteries, and all knowledge; and though I have all faith, so that I could remove mountains, and have not charity, I am nothing."

Being great in the sight of God does not consist in our being able to speak a variety of languages, but in using those languages for His glory by instructing believers and by bringing unbelievers to Christ.

The participles "prophesying" and "speaking" (*prophēteúōn* [4395] and *lalōn* [2980]) are in the present active nominative, which would indicate that the Apostle is referring, not so much to the mere historical fact of prophesying by a person, but to that person's ability, whether God-given or not, continuously to do so at will. He stresses the ability rather than the occurrence. When Paul writes about an individual who speaks on a particular occasion, he uses the singular form, "he that speaketh in a tongue"; but when he speaks about an individual in general who is endowed with this gift of languages, he properly uses the plural. "he that speaketh in tongues," for at one time one language and at another time a different language may be used by the same individual. The gift of being a linguist, as we have demonstrated and argued, seems to have been generally designated by the plural "tongues." And this gift, when consecrated to God, is of inestimable value in His service.

Edification Versus Boasting

Have you ever noticed the way some high school students just learning a foreign language like to show off by adding French, Latin, or Spanish phrases into the conversation? (They have some professors in their company, too.) They know full well these are incomprehensible to their listeners, but they cannot resist the temptation to demonstrate their superior knowledge to the confusion of younger brothers and sisters—or even parents! This may be amusing in youngsters, but it is childish to adults. If you are able to speak a foreign language and others do not understand it, you are not communicating your thoughts to them nor doing them any good.

Although Paul commended speaking in various languages as desirable, he stipulates that they must be languages that others understand. Speak to them in their language if you know it, and if you cannot do that, secure the services of an interpreter. Even if your motive is to display your command of a language, if it is unknown to your hearers, you should show them the consideration of interpreting for their benefit. That is the practical application of Paul's statement, "Greater is he that prophesieth than he that speaketh with tongues, except he interpret" (1 Cor. 14:5). Utilitarianism sometimes renders motivation less evil, at least as far as others are concerned, says Paul.

For believers to be able to speak in languages other than their own does not edify the congregation at all; but if they humbly surrender this ability to God, that He may use them as instruments to prophesy or witness, they are truly great. Not that Paul wants the Corinthians to strive for "greatness," but he is telling them that since greatness seems to be their aim, let it be true greatness. It is greater, then, to speak for the edification of others than to speak fluently in various languages, however great an accomplishment that may seem to them.

Except (*ei mē̂*)

Prophesying gives the greatest purpose to the use of any language. And whatever language you use, if it is unknown to any in the congregation that you are addressing, make sure that you interpret it. The expression *ei* (1487) *mē̂* (3361), "except" or "unless" in Greek, decides the point whether such a language should be used in public worship. Your first choice should be to use a language that most people in the assembly can understand. This may be a language foreign to yourself; it may be one of many foreign languages that you know; but if it is the one most generally understood, then prophesy in that. If there are those in the congregation who do not understand it, make sure that you interpret what you have said to them. The same person speaks in a foreign language and interprets it also. Paul is not engaged in a merely academic discussion here but is discussing the actual circumstances prevailing in the Corinthian church. How many languages were spoken in Corinth? The natives were Greek; the Roman conquerors spoke Latin; and the Jewish traders spoke Hebrew or Aramaic. There may have been other dialects also, but for the most part these were the languages spoken by the inhabitants of Corinth.

Let us suppose a case in point. Acts 18:7, 8 tells us that when Paul first came to Corinth he stayed at the home of Justus, whose house adjoined the synagogue. Crispus, the ruler of the synagogue, heard the gospel, believed, and was baptized. Now he is a member of the Corinthian congregation. Originally of Roman ancestry, he had become a Jew. He knows his native language, Italian or Latin, and also Hebrew, or he could not have become the chief ruler of the synagogue in Corinth. He must also know Greek, the native language of the Corinthian Greeks.

In other words, he is a polyglot. When he gets up to speak in the congregation, his purpose should be to prophesy, not just to speak in a language, any language. How can he best accomplish this? In his assembly he has Greeks, Jews, and Romans. Suppose that the majority are Greeks, which is quite likely, since there must have been more Greeks in Corinth than foreigners. Crispus now speaks in Greek, however, some of the Romans in his audience may not know neither Greek nor Hebrew. He will not disregard them. He must reach them, too, with the message. So after he speaks in Greek, he interprets what he has said in Latin. And if there are Jews present, he will interpret for them in Hebrew. This takes place in multilingual societies all the time. I am part of one. This is why this interpretation of what was happening in Corinth is so easy and natural for me to understand. But a monolinguist belonging to a society where only one language is spoken may never think of it. The Corinthian letters were written to those who were mostly polyglots.

This is what we may naturally presume to have happened all the time in Corinth. Many times I have had to do the same thing, speaking in two languages so that all in the congregation might understand what I was saying. And if there were some whose languages I did not know, another brother could usually be found who knew the language that I spoke and theirs also, so that he could interpret. Thus, the same person can translate, or someone else can undertake the task.

That (*hína*)

The purpose of such speaking is the edification of the church. And the expression of purpose is indicated by the Greek word *hína* (2443), which is much stronger here than a mere infinitive. (See the relevant comment in the previous chapter.) The purpose of whatever language we use should be prophesying, and the purpose of prophesying should be the edification of the local assembly, for this is what we understand Paul to mean by the term "church (*ekklēsía*, 1577)" here: "that the church may receive edifying."

Throughout the New Testament, the congregation, the local assembly of believers, is indicated as the central collective unit of God's concern. And indeed, the building up of the local branch of the Church of Jesus Christ where each of us worships should be our main concern. This is the Scriptural emphasis, and it should be ours. Let our concern not be how we can show off to best advantage in the local assembly, but what we can do to edify and build up that local assembly. There must be a conscious striving and sense of purpose in this. The Christian ought not to be motivated by what he can get out of his congregation, even in the matter of admiration for his natural or supernatural abilities, so much as by what he can do for the edification of his church. That should be his primary aim as part and parcel of the local assembly.

When Handel's oratorio of the "Messiah" had won the admiration of many of the great, Lord Kinnoul took occasion to pay him some compliments on the noble entertainment he had given the town lately. "My Lord," said Handel, "I should be sorry if I only entertained them; I wish to make them better." It is to be feared that many speech-makers at public meetings could not say as much. If we have nothing edifying to say, how much better to hold our tongue!

May Receive Edifying

In the clause, "that the church may receive edifying," the Greek word for "receive" is *lábē* (2983). This is in the second aorist active subjunctive tense (in the *hína* [2443] clause denoting purpose), referring to a historical action by way of emphasis rather than to a continuous process. It is as if Paul were saying that each time we prophesy in the local congregational meeting, even if it is in a foreign language, it must be for the purpose of edifying the church, not for self-glorification or even for personal edification alone without regard to others. How our church services would be revolutionized if we adhered strictly to this principle.

It is said of Pericles, the Athenian orator, that before he went out to address the people he used to pray that nothing might go out of his mouth but what might be to the purpose at hand. Here is a lesson for every Christian to take to heart before going forth to speak.

LESSONS:

1. Note here that Paul wrote "tongues" instead of "tongue." The KJV translators knew this, and that is why they did not insert "unknown" as an italicized word in this instance. The plural refers to the ability to speak God's wonders in non-native languages.

2. Do you wish that you could preach the gospel in several foreign languages? Are you failing to teach your next-door neighbor with English now?

3. Even if you were a skilled linguist but not utilizing this talent for God—only for self-serving purposes—what have you accomplished?

4. Paul wished that each of the Corinthians had the ability to speak in other foreign languages. However, Paul said that it was even more wonderful to use this gift to prophesy for the glory of God.

5. It is pointless to speak a foreign language to people who do not understand it. If that situation arises, Paul advised them to obtain a translator.

6. "Prophesying" allows the intent of the content to communicate successfully. The rule should be to adopt the particular language which will yield the greatest net understanding.

1 Cor. 14:6 | *What Is Profitable?*

Now, brethren, if I come unto you speaking with tongues, what shall I profit you, except I shall speak to you either by revelation, or by knowledge, or by prophesying, or by doctrine?

Think of Others When You Speak

Once again it should be noted that the primary purpose of speaking is to communicate our thoughts to others. This is the basic principle that the Apostle Paul elaborates in 1 Corinthians 14:6. In the Greek text, the verse begins with the words *nún* (3568) *dé* (1161), meaning "and now," indicating a transition from one argument to another. Until now, Paul had been using the third person in dealing with the matter of speaking in tongues. But now he proceeds to involve himself and those he addresses in the problem. It is as if he were saying, "And now let us come to grips with this. Suppose that I were to come to you" (as he most probably intended to do), "what would you expect of me?" Certainly they would expect his visit to be purposeful, and so would he.

It is easy to engage in academic discussions and feel that you are really solving problems and making intelligent decisions as to how things should be done. But put yourself into the thick of the problem before criticizing others or dictating solutions to situations you have never experienced. Suppose that you were the one involved. How would you behave; what would you do?

Paul disagreed with the Corinthians over their understanding of speaking in tongues. Yet observe how he treated them. He did not call them enemies of the gospel, the "lunatic fringe," "Holy Rollers," or any other derogatory name. He called them "brethren," the sweetest appellation in the Christian church. He wanted them to know that this matter was not so fundamental, so important, that communion and fellowship between them should be disrupted. Modern believers who profess to practice speaking in tongues exactly as the Corinthians of old did are sometimes treated with contempt by those who have Paul's enlightened understanding of the total question without his spirit of love. Certainly we need to learn of Paul, who, while differing with and correcting them, never ceased to be loving and tender. In the fourteenth chapter of his letter he practices what he preached in the thirteenth chapter. He admonishes them but he still calls them "brethren."

"If I come unto you speaking with tongues, what shall I profit you? . . ." he asks them. Now what tongues did he mean here? We really do not know whether they were human languages or ecstatic utterances, but it is obvious that they would be incomprehensible to the Corinthians. Most probably Paul was referring to their practice of speaking in non-human, non-understandable syllables when in an ecstatic mood. It is as if Paul were saying, "When I speak I do so in order to be understood; and if I come to you that is what you will want me to do, and that is what I will do. Why, then, do you keep up this practice of speaking in unknown tongues that the hearers cannot immediately comprehend? If I know the language of the majority, you will expect me, and I will expect, to speak in that language. If some of you do not understand me, there will at least be someone there who can translate, so that all may understand and be profited by my visit."

If I Come unto You Speaking

Logically, according to Paul's argument, the chief word in this question is not the verb *élthō* (2064), "I come," but the participle *lalōn* (2980), "speaking." Paul was not actually concerned with the fact of his going to Corinth. That was incidental to the argument. If he were to go, he would surely profit them a great deal by his very presence as well as by his instructions in the most holy faith. But this would not be so if he went in the fashion of one speaking with unknown tongues. Those who meet in this fashion today should consider this. The Apostle Paul was not willing to have a meeting just to speak in tongues. Are we more spiritually discerning than he? The force of his argument is, "What shall I profit you if I come to you and my primary behavior is that of speaking in one or more languages that you do not understand?" (a.t.). This is the principle that should guide all Christians when doing anything that involves others. Benefiting others should be the primary motivation of our behavior; especially should it be the basic concept of the task of the preacher, as it was of the Apostle Paul.

Paul has no doubt that he can be of benefit to the Corinthians in several ways, as he indicates, "either by revelation, or by knowledge, or by prophesying, or by doctrine." This is equivalent to the argument of the previous verse, where he places more importance on interpretation than on speaking in tongues. Interpretation is the vehicle of understanding. Revelation, knowledge, prophecy, and doctrine or teaching are four important elements that become known and useful to others through the tongue. Paul assumes himself the possessor of these things. He can only convey to the Corinthians what he himself has received. But how has he received revelation, knowledge, prophecy, and doctrine? Through hearing and understanding the teaching of the Holy Spirit, the Word of God, and of other Christians. If these had spoken to Paul in a language with which he was not familiar, he would never have understood any of the revelation of God; he would never have known anything of Christian doctrine; he would never have been able to prophesy and convey God's teaching to man.

By Revelation

It may be of help to consider briefly each of these four elements that Paul mentions. "Revelation" here indicates divine truth made known directly by God. What man cannot discover about God, man, and the universe had to be revealed to him by God. In Greek it is *apokalúpsis* (602), which literally means "taking off the lid, uncovering." There are things hidden from human understanding that God Himself has to uncover.

Or by Knowledge

"Knowledge" is incomplete without revelation. It is the preacher's duty to proclaim not only that which is humanly discoverable under God's providence but principally what is divinely revealed in a particular way unto salvation, and thus to show that all things that can be known consist in Christ. One first receives God's revelation, understands it, and then passes it on to others. All this is done through the medium of known, comprehensible language. Knowledge here is expressed by *gnōsis* (1108), which means "progressive knowledge, primarily of spiritual truth." Such knowledge can only be shared by the medium of speech.

Or by Prophesying, or by Doctrine

Prophecy and teaching are not possessions in the same sense as revelation and knowledge; they are activities. It is speech that converts revelation and knowledge into prophecy and teaching. Prophecy is telling forth what we know of God's revelation—whether of future events or, more usually, of the counsels of God, while teaching is more an elaboration of the declaration. Prophecy is concerned with giving forth the proposition, teaching with its explanation and proof. All this involves knowing what you are saying, Paul stresses.

Scripture tells us that whenever God spoke to man He did so in a language comprehensible to man to reveal Himself to man, to impart knowledge to man, to tell him of things that were to come, and to instruct him in His counsels. Paul desired to follow this divine example. He wanted to speak as God spoke, as clearly as he can. At Pentecost, when Peter spoke, he did so in the language understood by the majority of those present. The mere speaking was not as important as the understanding of what he was saying.

Revelation and knowledge, which are possessions, go together, whereas prophecy and teaching, which are activities, go together (see Lenski, R. H., *Interpretation of 1 and 2 Corinthians*. Minneapolis, MN: Augsburg Publishing House, 1971:583). No prophet can prophesy unless he has God's revelation; and no one can teach unless he himself knows his subject matter. Too many people try to prophesy without having received and understood God's revelation; too many try to teach without themselves knowing the thoughts and counsels of God. These four elements can stand alone or be coordinated. Take any of them—revelation, knowledge, prophecy, or teaching—and you will find them impossible without the medium of understandable speech. Speaking, therefore, does not exist for its own sake but has an underlying motive, to convey revelation, knowledge, prophecy, teaching. Speech has no inherent value; it is only an instrument to accomplish something beyond itself. Tongues, then, is actually not a gift at all, but a means to an end. Conveying thought, or knowledge, or revelation is what is important. Paul is speaking here about the congregation as a whole. He is concerned about the edification of the church (see vv. 4, 12). When we speak, we may be tempted to do so with certain individuals in mind whom we want to help or impress. But let us remember that the upbuilding of the entire local church should be the paramount object of the preacher's speech and preaching.

LESSONS:

1. Paul proposes a hypothetical example: "What if I were to come to you speaking a variety of foreign languages, none of which were known to you? And, suppose I made no effort to explain the meaning in your own language. What good would you get out of this exercise?"
2. Paul called these immature Christians "brethren." He did not ostracize them for these infantile behaviors.
3. Interpretation is the vehicle of understanding. Paul states that there are four ways to accomplish this: (1) revealing; (2) making something known progressively; (3) prophesying; and (4) teaching.

1 Cor. 14:7–10 | *Interpreted Sounds*

And even things without life giving sound, whether pipe or harp, except they give a distinction in the sounds, how shall it be known what is piped or harped? For if the trumpet give an uncertain sound, who shall prepare himself to the battle? So likewise ye, except ye utter by the tongue words easy to be understood, how shall it be known what is spoken? for ye shall speak into the air. There are, it may be, so many kinds of voices in the world, and none of them is without signification.

Sounds without Meaning

To convince the Corinthians that speaking in tongues unknown to the hearers is useless, Paul gives them an illustration from music. His argument runs as follows: You say that speaking in unknown tongues has some value. But would you enjoy hearing a pipe or harp by someone who knows no music and produces only noise? As Chrysostom said, "If things without life, supposing them to emit sound, are useless, unless they are guided by reason to give a distinction of sounds, much more may we expect this to be true of men, whose prerogative is reason." When you say that God speaks through you when you utter unintelligible sounds, Paul infers, it is like saying that God takes

31

up a harp and produces discord. This is an affront to His intelligence and purposefulness. Do not degrade Him to a place that you would consider beneath you.

Paul adds another illustration in verse 8. "For if the trumpet give an uncertain sound, who shall prepare himself to the battle?" The ancient war trumpet, though not strictly speaking an instrument of music, was used to produce distinctive sounds to summon troops and rouse their courage. Trumpet blasts become significant in consequence of a mutual understanding between the commander and his men. If the sound is uncertain, that is, if the meaning of the call is not previously agreed upon and understood, the trumpet is useless.

In verse 9, the Apostle proceeds to apply these illustrations. "So likewise ye, except ye utter by the tongue words easy to be understood, how shall it be known what is spoken? for ye shall speak into the air." The cumulative strength of the argument is this: If the military trumpet is more potent than pipe or lyre, still more expressive is the human tongue; but that also can produce sounds that convey no meaning. This is what he instructs the Corinthians to be careful about. "So also ye, unless by means of the tongue ye give speech that is distinct, how shall it be known what is spoken?" (a literal translation). The "tongue" here means the organ of speech, not the "ecstatic tongue" that never produced readily-comprehensible speech.

Easy to Be Understood

The expression translated "words easy to be understood" in verse 9 is *eúsēmon* (2154) *lógon* (3056) in Greek. The word *eúsēmon* comes from *eú* (2095, well) and *sēma* (4591, sign, mark, token). Our speech, says Paul, is a sign of something; the next word in Greek tells us of what. It is *lógon*, "word," which in use often means "intelligence" and also "expression." It is the same word that the Apostle John uses for the eternal name of the Lord

Jesus Christ. He is the Intelligence behind everything. "Before there was any beginning the Word had been" (John 1:1). The word *lógos* (3056) refers to expression that always has thought behind it. That is what our speech should be. Paul makes the transition from verse 8 to 9 of 1 Corinthians 14, by comparing lifeless musical instruments in verse 8, to animate, intelligent people in verse 9. If the pipe and the harp and the trumpet are made to give a melodious, meaningful sound, he argues, how much more you who are possessed with intelligence?

So Likewise Ye

"So likewise ye, except ye utter by the tongue words easy to be understood [that is, a good sign of reason or thought], how shall it be known what is spoken? for ye shall speak into the air." The Corinthians did not speak in unknown tongues simply; they wanted to speak in an unknown language merely for self-gratification and to demonstrate that they were filled with the Holy Spirit. It was a selfish purpose, and Paul exposes it as such.

Many Kinds of Voices in the World

Paul then continues his argument against this purposeless speaking in verse 10, where he says, "There are, it may be, so many kinds of voices in the world, and none of them is without signification." The expression "many kinds" is *géne* (1085), the same word Paul uses at the end of verse 28 in the twelfth chapter. It means species, varieties, families of voices. Paul says that there are a variety of voices as there are a variety of tongues. He does not claim to know all of them, as evidenced by the Greek expression *ei* (1487) *túchoi* (5177), which may be better rendered "if it should happen" or by way of paraphrase "I dare say." It implies that the number is large, but that the exact number does not matter. "There are, I dare say, ever so many varieties of voices."

This is what Paul is saying to the Corinthians: Those who hear you know whether you are speaking in an intelligent human language, whatever variety it belongs to (and these are many), or whether you are producing meaningless sounds. And he adds, "And none of them is without ." Actually in the Greek it is "and none," referring not to the voice (*phōnē*, 5456) but to the *génē* (1085) (varieties). "And no variety of voices is voiceless" is the literal meaning. What he is trying to prove to the Corinthians is that their tongue-speaking is not humanly distinguishable as a variety of languages and therefore cannot be truly interpreted. The interpreter can only guess at what is being said, in which case the interpreter becomes the prophet and the person who speaks nothing. There is thus some value in the interpretation in such circumstances but none in the tongue-speaking.

Without Signification

The use of the word *áphōnon* (880), "voiceless," referring to a family of voices, is peculiar to this passage. How can a voice or a group of voices be voiceless? This is a figure of speech known as an oxymoron, frequently used in Greek, an expression combining contradictory words for epigrammatic effect, such as "an unlivable life," "joyless joy," and so forth. Paul actually classifies the Corinthian tongue-speaking as a variety of voices. It constitutes a family of speech, although it has no homogeneity. These unknown tongues cannot be broken down into uniform phonetic sounds that can have the same consistent meaning each time they are uttered. There are phonetic sounds that actually constitute a whole science of linguistics that the expert translators of the Bible societies and the Wycliffe Bible Translators can recognize. Whenever these experts have had the opportunity to hear modern Corinthians speaking in unknown tongues, they have not been able to break them down into consistent phonetic sounds, which is an indication that they are not the product of intelligent thinking for the purpose of conveying meaning. When you want "bread," for instance, you always use the same word when asking for it. Each object or idea has a particular consistent word to express it in human language; but this is not the case with the varieties of tongue-speaking. A "voiceless voice," therefore, is a meaningless voice; and to employ it is below the dignity of man and of God, who made man far superior to soulless musical instruments. If we do not use such instruments to produce meaningless sounds, we should not of our own volition speak with meaningless voices, nor should we think that God would allow us to do so. Speech without meaning is a contradiction of terms!

LESSONS:

1. Would you enjoy hearing someone play an instrument of music? What if they did not know how to play it? How long would you listen to the cacophony?
2. If an ancient war trumpet did not emit a clear-cut, distinctive sound, then the troops would not be mustered. In other words, a meaningless sound would produce confusion between the commander and his fighting men.
3. The human tongue has more potential to evoke meaning than the simple signal of a trumpet. Conversely, the potential for bedlam is proportionately greater when the gift of meaningful speech is abused.
4. There are a variety of voices (sounds, *phōnân* [5456]), just as there are a variety of languages. Though you may not understand them all, each one of them is meaningful (phonemic, morphological, and syntactic).

1 Cor. 14:11 | *Barbarism (Uncivilized)*

Therefore if I know not the meaning of the voice, I shall be unto him that speaketh a barbarian, and he that speaketh shall be a barbarian unto me.

In 1 Corinthians 16:5–7 Paul expresses his earnest wish to be in Corinth, believing he will be there soon. Not only does he have a great desire to be with the Corinthians, but he also wants to be useful among them. Part of his usefulness depends on his ability to speak to the Corinthians in a way that they will be able to understand him. "Now, brethren," Paul said in 1 Corinthians 14:6, "if I come unto you speaking with tongues [foreign, untranslated languages], what shall I profit you, except [*eán* {1437}, if, and *mē* {3361}, not] I shall speak to you either by revelation, or by knowledge, or by prophesying, or by doctrine?" Paul continued to desire their understanding of his teaching even after he taught them. We find proof of this in 2 Corinthians 16:20, 21 where Paul expresses his fear that in returning to the Corinthians, he will find them unchanged.

Paul first uses the hypothetical "if" (*eán*) in 1 Corinthians 14:6. In verse 7 of the same chapter he uses it a second time. Here Paul uses it to indicate that we even try to discern meaning from listening to musical instruments by assigning significance to the sounds we hear. For instance, we regulate the sound of a pipe through shaping our mouths in particular ways to blow certain amounts of air into it. Then as someone listens to the sound of our pipe, they will attribute meaning to its sound according to the way we have shaped our mouths to produce it. The word is *phthóggos* (5353), a shaped sound meaningful to the ear. The verb *phthéggomai* (5350) is related to the noun *apophthéggomai* (669) which is used only twice, in Acts 2:4, 14, and is translated in the King James Version "to give utterance" and "say." Furthermore rooted in the meaning of *apophthéggomai* (669) is the aspect of meaningful speech. Such speech is evident in the manifestation of languages spoken at Pentecost.

The tongues spoken at Pentecost were human languages that needed no interpretation to be understood. They were dialects *(diálektoi* [1258], languages; Acts 2:6, 8), a term never used regarding the unknown tongue of the Corinthian practice in 1 Corinthians 14. Paul also used the compound verb *apophthéggomai* in his defense speech before Festus in Acts 26:25 when he said, "I speak forth [*apophthéggomai*] the words of truth and soberness." Festus could directly understand them.

The meaningful sound of the flute is not an indiscriminate blowing of air, but in 1 Corinthians 14:7 is called *auléō* (832), to harp, that is to play the pipe or harp. Playing an instrument to create a meaningful sound takes intelligence and ability as well as training and discipline. Certainly opening and closing one's mouth and blowing to produce sounds is not enough to convey a significant message. If a person has enough sense to know that and instead demonstrates intelligence and ability in playing the flute or harp, how much more should he use intelligently that unique instrument of sound, the tongue, which the Lord built into the body.

BARBARISM (UNCIVILIZED)

"Therefore, if I Know [Realize]"

In verse 11 Paul uses the hypothetical "if" (*eán*) for the third time in this chapter. What is translated "I know" (KJV) is the Greek word *eidō* (1492), the first person singular perfect active subjunctive of *eídō*, used with the present meaning and derived from the verb *eídō*, to know, to recognize.

Unfortunately, the inadequacy of the translations of the New Testament is partly due to the failure to distinguish the various forms of this verb *eídō* as meaning to know intuitively, to recognize, versus the verb *ginṓskō*, (1097) to know by acquisition, to learn. One may learn music, but only after one studies it does he or she acquire the ability to make meaningful sounds. Each note, if you realize what it is, has meaning which will indicate an action. The verb then in verse 11 is *eídō*, to recognize musical sounds. And when one becomes a child of God, he recognizes the voice of God.

"Not the Meaning of the Voice"

When one speaks, there is intonation in the voice which is significant. My wife would always tell our children, "It is not what you say that is important; it is how you say it." If I say something angrily, others consider me angry; if I say something pleadingly, their impression is that I am weak; if I say it as a command, they find me superior in appearance.

In the Greek text the noun is *dúnamis* (1411), accomplishing power. It is necessary to recognize or realize the meaning of the voice so that it may accomplish its purpose. The word *dúnamis* stands in contrast to the synonymous noun *ischús* (2479), inherent power, strength. There is meaning to the intonation of the voice.

BARBARISM (UNCIVILIZED)

"I Shall Be to the One Who Speaketh a Barbarian"

A barbarian here has reference to the one who did not speak the Greek language during that particular era and was thus unintelligible to the inhabitants of Greece. As W. F. Boyd says in James Hasting's *Dictionary of the Apostolic Church:*

> The word itself is almost certainly onomatopoetic, being an imitation of the way in which the people seem to speak. It occurs for the first time in Homer (1. 2. 867), and is used of the Carians who were called *barbaróphōnoi* (speaking like barbarians). Plato divides the human race into Hellenes and Barbarians (Polit. 262 D). Even the Romans called themselves Barbarians till Greek literature came to be naturalized in Rome; and both Philo and Josephus regard the Jews and their tongue as Barbarians. By and by, the word came to be used as descriptive of all the defects which the Greeks thought foreign to themselves and natural to all other peoples, but the first and the main idea conveyed by the terms is that of difference of language.

Here Paul refers to the person in Corinth who speaks in a manner incomprehensible to the hearer. To such a person anyone listening will be a barbarian, that is, uncivilized, incapable of comprehending. Therefore, the person who speaks in either an unknown tongue or a foreign language without a translator is emboldened to regard the hearer as ignorant or uncivilized.

"And He Who Speaketh Shall Be a Barbarian to Me"

If I listen to such a person, I shall be considered a barbarian, and if I speak I shall also be a barbarian. Either as a listener or as a speaker, I am the same—a barbarian—if I do not use a meaningful language.

LESSONS:

1. Sounds made by men ought to be meaningful—not just noise.
2. Voices have "powers." They cause those who hear them to do certain things.

Barbarism (Uncivilized)

LESSONS:

1. Sounds made by men ought to be meaningful—not just noise.
2. Voices have "powers." They cause those who hear them to do certain things.
3. Even the intonation of the voice has meaning.
4. If I am among people whose language I do not understand, I will be considered ignorant.
5. If I speak in an unknown tongue or language to others who cannot understand, I am uncivilized.

BARBARISM (UNCIVILIZED)

1 Cor. 14:12 | *Spirituality Means Edification*

Even so ye, forasmuch as ye are zealous of spiritual gifts,
seek that ye may excel to the edifying of the church.

In verse 9 Paul tells the Corinthians that they should neither listen to meaningless noises nor speak them, for even musical instruments should convey meaningful sounds that lead to action. If they do not, others will come to the conclusion that they are uncivilized or barbarians.

"Even so Ye"

Now again, as in verse 9, Paul says, "Even so ye." He acknowledges the possibility of the Corinthians having a spiritual motive. But, he cautions them to take time to look at the conclusion which they and others must come to as a result of their practice of speaking in an unknown tongue or incomprehensible languages.

Paul now draws a second conclusion regarding speaking in an unknown tongue. It is that in the endeavor to be spiritual, the Corinthians should be sure that they are, in actuality, edifying the church. If they are not edifying it, then they are not demonstrating spirituality in spite of their supposition.

Paul explains that as harmony and pleasurable hearing are the desired results of musical notes, so also should the spiritual edification of the church be the believer's goal. Before producing meaningful musical notes a musician checks his instrument to be certain it is in tune. In the same way, Christians should examine themselves to be sure that they are spiritually in tune with God.

"Inasmuch as You Are Zealous of Spiritual Gifts"

This phrase begins with the conjunction *epeí* (1893), inasmuch. It is a hypothetical conjunction made up of the preposition *epí* (1909), upon, and the conditional conjunction *ei* (1487), which is the subjective "if." Let us suppose, Paul says, that you are in pursuit of "spirits [*pneumátōn* {4152}]." He does not say that these Corinthians are seeking the Holy Spirit, but simply "spirits." In 1 John 4:1 we are advised "not to believe every spirit, but to try the spirits whether they are of God: because many false prophets are gone out into the world." One of God's gifts is the "discerning of spirits" (1 Cor. 12:10).

The King James Version translates *pneumátōn* (4151), of spirits, as "of spiritual gifts." The word "gifts" has been added in the English translation, and because it is not in the Greek text it is in italics. In the Greek text, Paul speaks of "spirits" and not of "spiritual gifts" which would have been *charismátōn* (5486). The Corinthians desired spiritual experiences such as speaking in an unknown tongue. But if speaking in an unknown tongue was a truly spiritual experience, it would have been the result of the Holy Spirit and would bring order and propriety. The same qualities which characterize God also characterize the Holy Spirit.

The word translated "zealous" in Greek is *zēlōtaí* (2207), eagerly desirous. This is the only time Paul uses this adjectival noun in this epistle. He is not commending the Corinthians for their spirituality which would be contrary to his characterization of them throughout this epistle. In 1 Corinthians 3:1 he wrote to them "And I, brethren, could not speak unto you as unto spiritual, but as unto carnal [*sarkikoí* {4559} which is the opposite of *pneumatikoí*, spiritual] even as unto babes in Christ."

Let us not fail to realize that the conjunction *epeí* means "inasmuch as if." This "if" is the hypothetical conjunction *ei*: Even so as if you were, we would say in English. Paul cannot call the Corinthians "carnal babies" in 1 Corinthians 3:1 and then in 14:12 refer to them as "zealots" of the Holy Spirit. They were zealots of spirits or spiritual things, deceiving themselves. They were carnal, complaining babies, but thinking themselves to be adults praising God, and behaving like children playing church This is the same deception that has crept into our praise services today when we repeat over and over again as though God did not hear us the first time! We act as if we are praising a deaf God, and so we repeat our praise until it becomes trite.

Of all the glorious experiences Paul recounts of himself, there is none to equal that which he speaks about in 2 Corinthians 12:1–10. He was in reality caught up into paradise, and it was so glorious that he did not know whether the experience was actually a bodily experience or was purely spiritual. But the Lord did not want him to mention it more than three times. His was a real experience, although perhaps "in the spirit." The Corinthians were caught up in a frenzy which they misunderstood to be the zeal invoked by the Holy Spirit whereas it was by "spirits."

They even misunderstood Paul's message when he spoke to them in that unparalleled hymn of love in 1 Corinthians 13. Oh, for the true understanding of this verse, "Thus you also, inasmuch as you are zealous of spirits. . . ." No doubt you are motivated by spiritual interest, Paul advises, but recognize that it is not the Holy Spirit, for if it were, the result of your spiritual activity would have been the edification of the church. Paul takes it for granted that everybody knows this has not been so. We merely need to read 1 Corinthians 1:12–17 to find out that the Corinthian church was schismatic.

Paul began this chapter by saying to the Corinthians, "Pursue [*diṓkete* {1377}] the love [of which he wrote in chapter 13], and be zealous about spiritual matters [*tá pneumatiká*], but rather that you may prophesy" (1 Cor. 14:1). Because the King James Version translators added the word "gifts" after the word "spiritual," it was assumed that it should also be added after *pneumátōn*, of spirits in 1 Corinthians 14:12. In my opinion this was the wrong assumption, for *pneúmata*, spirits, is not *pneumatiká* (spiritual) gifts. If the Corinthians were guided by the Holy Spirit or spiritual gifts, the result would have been the edification of their church, which was not the case. Their practices brought division, not peace and joy and love. These were the things in which they should have sought to excel.

"Seek That You May Excel"

"Seek" is the Greek *zēteíte*, the second person plural present active imperative of *zētéō* (2212), to seek. The verb is followed by the conjunction *hína* (2443), in order that, which indicates purpose.

The purpose the Corinthians were to seek should have been to excel in the edification of the church. "To excel" renders the Greek verb *perisseúēte*, the second person plural present active subjunctive of *perisseúō* (4052), to abound. This would mean to have enough for oneself and an overflow so that the satisfaction would flow over to others.

The tendency of some is to be active in a church for the benefit they may receive for themselves. Very few of us join a church for the primary purpose of the blessing and edification we can impart to others. The verb *perisseúō*, to abound, does not mean to neglect ourselves, but to be satisfied with as little or as much as God sends our way and to make it suffice not only to meet our needs, but also to meet the needs of others. When the Lord fed the 5,000 plus and the 4,000 plus, He did not supply only the basic necessity of those who were there, but in each case there was a surplus which was not allowed to go to waste (Matt. 14:20; 15:37). In 2 Corinthians 9:8 Paul says, "And God is able to make all grace abound [*perisseúō*] toward you; that you, always having all sufficiency [*autárkeia* {841}, self-sufficiency, self-satisfaction, contentedness] in all things, may abound [*perisseúō*] to every good work."

Now in the practice of speaking in an unknown tongue, the common argument by those who exercised it was that "it made them feel spiritual," thus good because they were speaking to God—this in spite of the fact that no one could understand them. This was a total disregard of others. The time spent listening to someone speak in a language which could not be understood could have been more effectively utilized in encouragement, comfort, and the teaching of the Scriptures.

Note 1 Corinthians 14:2: "For he that speaks in an unknown tongue speaks not unto men, but unto God: for no man understands him; howbeit in the spirit he speaks mysteries." Note that the word "spirit" is written with a lowercase "s," not with a capital one as is the Holy Spirit. The Corinthians mistook their own spirit as the Holy Spirit, while the fact is that the Holy Spirit is never named in 1 Corinthians 14 (vv. 2, 12, 14 which says "my spirit," 15, 16, 32). The Holy Spirit does not motivate a selfish environment. Whenever He gives anything, He causes it to abound (*perisseúō*) for it satisfies not only self, but others also. That is why, speaking of the coming of the Holy Spirit, Jesus said that He was going to cause those who receive Him to become "witnesses" (*mártures* [3140]). In order to be a witness, others must be able to understand what is being said, for others are not edified if one speaks only to God. Nor does God need to be addressed in an unknown tongue for He knows all. He knows even our thoughts and attitudes (Matt. 6:32).

"To the Edification of the Church"

For this reason we find a marked distinction drawn by the Apostle Paul between speaking in an unknown tongue and prophesying; thus, if a choice is to be made, prophesying is to be preferred for "he who prophesies speaks unto men to edification [*oikodomē* {3619}, the same word as in 1 Cor. 14:12], and exhortation, and comfort." Paul said in 1 Corinthians 14:19, "Yet in the church I had rather speak five words with my understanding, that by my voice I might teach others also, than ten thousand words in an unknown tongue."

The conclusion of the matter, therefore, is that he who speaks in an unknown tongue does not speak for the benefit of others, but for his own benefit. He or she is not motivated to do so, through the exercise of spiritual gifts, but through a selfish and prideful motive emanating from his own spirit. This can be a desire to show how close to God a person is or a feeling of superiority because he or she has this special "gift" of God. When one is genuinely close to God, he will not be satisfied fully until the grace of God in Christ overflows (*perisseúō*) to others who are eager to share in the surplus of His provision.

LESSONS:

1. Verse 12 must be taken as built on the subjective supposition introduced by the Greek conjunction *epeí* which is derived from *epí*, upon, and *ei*, if, inasmuch as, thus "if you are zealous of spirits."
2. By "spirits" in this verse, Paul does not refer to the spiritual gifts he enumerates in 1 Corinthians 12:4–11. In this latter passage he does not classify the practice of speaking in an unknown tongue as a gift of grace (*chárisma*), but the gift graced by God to know the families of languages and the ability to interpret them.

3. If the practice of speaking in an unknown tongue came from the Holy Spirit, it would result in the edification of the church.
4. It was Paul's wish that many should be used for the edification of the church of Corinth, but to be so used they should not seek to satisfy themselves but others.

1 Cor. 14:13–15 | *Understanding*

*Wherefore let him that speaketh in an unknown tongue
pray that he may interpret. For if I pray in an unknown
tongue, my spirit prayeth, but my understanding is unfruitful. What is it then? I will pray with the spirit, and
I will pray with the understanding also: I will sing with
the spirit, and I will sing with the understanding also.*

Use Your Head and Heart Together

Paul has established that the primary purpose of speech is
communication of thought, and in public worship it is the edification of the local church. In order for a man to be edified he
must understand what is spoken. Understanding is the important thing and not speech per se. Having established this indisputable fact, Paul proceeds to give a piece of advice: "Wherefore
let him that speaketh in an unknown tongue pray that he may interpret" (1 Cor. 14:13).

Wherefore

The "wherefore" presupposes a concession on Paul's part. Because
of the insistence of these Corinthians that ecstatic speaking
seems to do them good, that it is a gratifying experience although
merely emotional, Paul does not dictatorially insist that they shall

stop it altogether. Instead he makes recommendations that will persuade them that it is wrong and cause them to quit on their own. This is sound psychology. To tell people not to do something is seldom as effective as showing them the unhappy results of their actions, thus motivating them to decide for themselves that it is not worthwhile. This is a good principle to remember when you seek to correct someone in the Christian congregation.

Paul here implies that the ability to interpret an unknown tongue is the factor that makes speaking with tongues tolerable, with the further implication that if you can interpret why should you not speak in an understandable language to begin with? If you cannot interpret, the claim that what you have is a gift of the Holy Ghost is certainly open to question. You are only deceiving yourself if you think that you have the historic gift of tongues manifested at Pentecost, Caesarea, and Ephesus, for in these instances the hearers comprehended them immediately. It is also very questionable that you are speaking an angelic language, since angels are never recorded as speaking to men in a language that was not understood by men.

Paul is more interested here in the net result of this practice than in the process itself. "I have no objection," he says, "to your speaking in tongues as long as you also have the ability to interpret so that others may understand you" (a.t.). Since speaking with a tongue is not a human language, but is supposed to be the language of heaven, it would have to be a distinct revelation from God. Therefore, the interpretation would also have to come directly from God, and this requires prayer to Him. Hence, the irony of Paul's advice: You need a double revelation—one for speaking in an unknown tongue and one for interpreting it. The implication is this: Why would God go to all this trouble? Why could He not reveal the meaning without the tongues in the first place, since the meaning of the revelation is the important thing for others?

UNDERSTANDING

If I Pray

In verse 14 Paul explains why he gave the advice in verse 13, to pray for the ability to interpret what you say, if neither you nor anyone else can understand it. He says, "For if I pray in an unknown tongue, my spirit prayeth, but my understanding is unfruitful." When you pray for the ability to interpret, pray understandingly and not in an unknown tongue. Such prayer involves the understanding. This is the prayer of verse 13. But in verse 14, we have a different kind of prayer, the prayer in an unknown tongue. Paul says, "Suppose I were to pray in an unknown tongue. I would not know what I was saying." (This presupposes that he does not have the ability to interpret because if he did he would know for what he was praying and the ultimate purpose of prayer would be accomplished because he asked intelligently.) "Here I am," he says, "praying with meaningless sounds, and as a result I do not know what I am saying nor does anybody else. My spirit prays, but my understanding is unfruitful." Paul does not say that he does this; he merely supposes it in order to teach the Corinthians how misguided this practice is, even in prayer. The context of this is still the local assembly of believers, as the verse sixteen clearly indicates.

My Spirit

The word spirit here cannot possibly mean the Holy Spirit. The personal pronoun "my" clearly indicates this. Remember that not once is the Holy Spirit spoken of in 1 Corinthians 14 in connection with speaking in unknown tongues. It is my spirit and my understanding, says Paul. The immaterial part of man's being is what he refers to here, that through which God communicates with him. But in verses 13 and 14 the word spirit emphasizes also the spirit as the seat of the emotions in the immediate context. Since God is Spirit, man can only communicate with Him and receive His message through his spirit. There must always be a correspondence between the transmitter and the receiver, even as our radios must be tuned to the proper wave length of the transmitting station. What Paul is saying here is that communication between God and man is possible without audible speech. The deaf and mute can communicate with God. This is praying with one's spirit. Paul is not denying that this can be done.

My Understanding

But man has a further ability, he says, and that is the active reason, the thinking mind, the process of the understanding, the *noús* (3563), as he designates it in the Greek text. The spirit originates and governs the *noús*. *Noús* is a capacity or process of the spirit. "But my understanding is unfruitful." The word *ákarpos* (175), "unfruitful," implies that the mind (*noús*) may be active in constructive planning, and this consequently leads to fruitful accomplishments on the part of the thinker. The Lord gave me my mind in order to use it at all times; if I do not use it, it is deprived of its intended function of producing distinct thoughts that will benefit others. But speaking with an unknown tongue bypasses intelligence. Beware of any action of the spirit that ignores the God-given faculty of thinking. God did not intend either faculty to be put aside at will. He intended mind and spirit to be actively coordinated, to bear fruit for God in affecting the lives of others.

The spirit of man in this instance stands also for his spirit as the seat of his emotions. I can be emotional without actively engaging my mind, and even receive great blessing as a result of such an experience, but it is not God's highest intent for me. That is why in verse 15 Paul says, "I will pray with the spirit, and I will pray with the understanding also: I will sing with the spirit, and I will sing with the understanding also." He did not mean that at one time he would pray and sing with his emotions only, and at others with his mind also. He meant both together and complementing each other. This is what is pleasing to God.

Observe the order of these two elements of prayer: spirituality precedes intelligence. We must first believe and then we shall know. The spirit of man is also the seat of his faith as well as of his emotions. Although both are activities of a man's spirit, they must not be confused. Modern man generally wants intellectual comprehension to precede faith. But this is not the Biblical order. We must remember that the raw material of prayer is not its intellectual content, but our feelings of love, and moral persuasion. Undoubtedly, earnest prayer is often compatible with a very slight exercise of the understanding, as was the case with the Corinthians whom Paul endeavors to correct. This was the practice but not the ideal. This was actually the state to which the Corinthians had brought themselves as they spoke in tongues. They were capable of thinking while they spoke and yet they did not; they preferred to rattle off unknown sounds that could not be reduced to intelligent words and thoughts. Paul's plea therefore is for these Corinthians to supply guidance to their emotions.

In order to show the interaction of emotion and thought in worship, the Apostle announces his resolution as to how he will behave in the house of God. "What is it then? I will pray with the spirit, and I will pray with the understanding also: I will sing with the spirit, and I will sing with the understanding also." Whether praying, singing, or preaching (see v. 19), Paul is determined to use both his God-given faculties: his own spirit and his own mind.

LESSONS:

1. Throughout the fourteenth chapter of 1 Corinthians, Paul places a great premium upon comprehension. Without it edification cannot take place.

2. Paul seeks to persuade the Corinthian Christians to refrain from glossolalia by showing them its unhappy fruits.

3. If this practice were truly from God, there would have to be a double revelation—(1) the vociferation in the "unknown" tongue; (2) the inspired interpretation of the message in (1).

4. Paul is stating that if someone were praying in an "unknown" tongue, then that individual would not know what he was saying. Why pray with meaningless sounds which are not understood by the praying person or by anyone else? That would not make any sense!

5. The Lord gave your mind (*nous*, 3563) to you to use at all times. If you repeatedly put your mind "in neutral," you will eventually lose the use of it altogether. Head and heart must be together, and neither should be confused.

1 Cor. 14:16

Responding

Else when thou shalt bless with the spirit, how shall he that occupieth the room of the unlearned say Amen at thy giving of thanks, seeing he understandeth not what thou sayest?

What about the Hearers?

Paul has just finished illustrating a point by supposing himself to be in the place of the Corinthians who were speaking in unknown tongues. He did not actually mean that there were times when he prayed only with his spirit or sang with his spirit without using his mind. He was placing himself in the position of the Corinthians, as shown by the fact that in verses 16 and 17 he shifts from the first person to the second person, from "I" to "you." Therefore, in all these verses, from 14 to 17, we must presuppose the term "for instance." "Take myself, for instance," or "Now take yourselves, for instance." His argument is, Suppose in your case we say that, when you speak in tongues, you are really praying or singing with your spirits only. Since we have agreed that the primary purpose of public worship is the edification of the entire assembly of believers, let us see whether your practice of praying with the spirit only, without giving direction through your mind to your emotions, is accomplishing the desired purpose, the edification of the local church.

Else When

Verse 16 in the KJV begins, "Else, when." In the Greek text it is *epeí* (1893) *eán* (1437), literally "for if," and is equivalent to "otherwise." Again the gentle spirit of the Apostle Paul continues to say "if" instead of involving himself in a direct rebuke to these Corinthians. He does this not only to make them understand their own fault and correct themselves, but to prevent any possible misunderstanding that it is possible for them to bless with their spirits only without using their minds. Therefore, he puts it as a supposition, "For if when you bless with your spirit." We must be careful not to jump to wrong conclusions from certain portions of Scripture by taking suppositions to be commands and facts when they are merely intended as illustrations. The Apostle Paul is not saying to these Corinthians, "When you speak with unknown tongues, you are blessing with your spirit." Nothing of the kind. He is saying, "Suppose that when you speak with tongues you bless with your spirit only—what then?" This is a mere supposition, predicated on the assumption that it is possible for one to pray with the spirit only without the understanding; and it is to be remembered that this is what he condemned in the two previous verses.

Thou Shalt Bless

The Greek word used here for "bless" is *eulogēs* (2127), from which we get the English word "eulogize," basically meaning "to speak well of." This is often used to express thanks or praise directed toward a person or speaking of a person. Paul still has in mind here the audible words of one who is praying in public. Suppose you are saying something good about God, or your fellow believers, or some blessing God has brought about in your life, he suggests. Is this possible in the first place without the use of your mind? Such "eulogizing" involves a recognition of the distinction between what is good and what is bad, what is a blessing and what is a curse. The ability to make moral distinctions belongs to the faculty of the mind, which is God-given.

Furthermore, the Greek word *eulogḗs* (2127) is a compound word including *lógos* (3056), which means "word," then "reason, intelligence." It is the same word from which we get "logician" and "logic," and which designates the name of the Lord Jesus Christ in the first eighteen verses of the gospel of John as the Intelligence, eternal and infinite, that gave birth to everything. The very word, then, that the Apostle Paul uses involves the faculty of thought, of reason, of intelligence. Thus, indirectly he shows how impossible it is to bless God, or to eulogize God or man, without using one's mind. He wants to persuade these Corinthians fully that the two operations—that of the spirit, standing here for the seat of the emotional aspect of man, and that of the mind (*lógos, noús* [3563]), standing for man's reasoning ability—should work together in recognizing the goodness of God and His activity in our lives, as well as in recognizing what is good or bad in the lives of others.

The Unlearned

This verse in no way indicates that there were special places reserved for the unlearned. Paul has in mind that some in the congregation will be advanced Christians, who are well-informed about the Scriptures and the doctrine of Christ, and those who are yet unlearned. It is the latter who may be scandalized by such manifestations of ecstasy. We, too, should exhibit Paul's concern about these immature believers. The word translated "the unlearned" in Greek is *idiṓtou* (2399), which in its primary sense means "a layman, a person who occupies a private position in contradistinction to an official of some kind, or one who lacks technical or expert knowledge in contradistinction to an expert in some special line; hence in a broad sense a layman." In no way does this passage of Scripture indicate that there were reserved seats for either learned or unlearned. Paul indicates concern about those who have just believed or who are still investigating to determine whether or not to believe the gospel of Jesus Christ. In public worship and in private life, we Christians should behave in fear and trembling lest we become stumbling-blocks to such people.

How can such a layman, inexperienced in spiritual things, possibly say "Amen" to such unintelligible utterances, since he does not understand what you are saying? Again Paul drives home the futility of speaking with tongues without making their meaning known. "Amen" is a transliterated Hebrew word for "truth" or "verity," and is used in Greek as well as in many other languages to express full and decided assent. One cannot agree or disagree with something unless he understands it. Therefore, we have one more evidence that the speaking with tongues referred to in this passage, as practiced by the Corinthians was not speaking in an understandable language for the purpose of making the counsels of God known to those present at the place of worship, but was ecstatic utterance emotionally induced.

Giving of Thanks

It is evident in verse 16 that the word "bless" in Greek ("eulogize") and the word "giving of thanks" are synonymous. The Christian who speaks in tongues apparently is so filled with the joy of the Lord for His blessing upon his life that his spirit indulges in an emotional outburst of thanksgiving. But as you express your thanksgiving to God in public worship, remember that you must give the opportunity to advanced Christians, to beginners, and to those who are still seekers, to know the reason for your thanksgiving so that they may give their assent that God is indeed worthy to be praised.

Paul concedes in verse 17 that such ecstatic thanksgiving is good for the person who gives it, but not for the other person because he is not edified by it. "For thou verily givest thanks well, but the other is not edified." The word for "other" here is the Greek *héteros* (2087), meaning generally "another of a different quality." (See Trench, p. 357ff.) We must be considerate of those who are qualitatively different from us in their Christian make-up. The Apostle Paul makes a plea for those who speak in unknown tongues, even in their thanksgiving to God, to be governed, not by whether their thanksgiving is good in itself or does them good, but whether it is upbuilding to someone whose spiritual make-up is different from theirs or who has had no spiritual experience whatever. This is a basic Christian principle, not only in the matter of speaking in tongues, but in all our conduct as Christians. Try it when you are in doubt about smoking, drinking, dancing, or other things that could conceivably affect others besides yourself.

LESSONS:

1. The Apostle Paul is saying: "Well, Corinthians, let's operate with your assumptions for awhile. Suppose when you are 'speaking in tongues' (i.e. praying or singing only with your spirits), since you and I have already agreed that edification of the whole group is the primary purpose of public worship, does tongue-speaking really help people?"
2. Common people deserve to be communicated with in ordinary language which they can easily understand. The Master understood this principle; He used parables to speak with the people "as they were able to hear it" (Mark 4:33).

| 1 Cor. 14:17 | *Consideration of Others* |

For you verily givest thanks well, but the other is not edified.

When one speaks in an unknown tongue, he is considering his own relationship with God only. It is likely that he may be thanking God for blessings and answers to prayer. This in itself is commendable.

"For You Verily Givest Thanks Well"

"You," Paul says, "on the one hand [*mén* {3303}, translated 'verily' in the KJV] give thanks well [*kalôs* {2573}]." Actually, one does not have to say anything to express gratitude to the Lord. A silent prayer of thanksgiving is possible, and even a grateful attitude is pleasing to God. However, it is instructive to express it with words. A child of God can speak to his Lord in his own language even when no one else understands it. But we can be sure that God does.

Such thanksgiving has a special word in Greek. It is the verb *eucharistéō* (2168). This word means that you are telling God that you are well pleased with His grace which you received. The word begins with *eu* (2095), good or well as the prefix, and the noun *cháris* (5485), grace, which is God's unmerited favor. When you are thanking God, you are telling Him that His favor is well received by you.

A prayer of thanksgiving, however, becomes more precious when it is shared with someone else in the congregation. That someone else may be different than the one praying, and this we determine from the Greek word *héteros* (2087), meaning one who is different.

In our thanksgiving in public we may not think that we are influencing others, but it is surprising how much we do influence them. There are those who will say "Amen" as they hear us give thanksgiving (v. 16). They agree with us that the things that we are thankful for ought to arouse gratitude, and they will be encouraged in their faith and in their prayer life. But there are those who are different and will be impressed that we thank the Lord for difficulties also, for instead of complaining, we give thanks.

The adverb "well" (*kalōs* [2573]) could be interpreted as meaning that you thank the Lord for the things that are obviously well received, which constitute the common good or common blessings. You may thank the Lord for food, clothes, friends, health, or prosperity. Everyone is thankful for such blessings, although there are those who neglect to thank God from whom all blessings flow. But how impressed the others worshiping the Lord are when they hear a believer thank God even in afflictions as the Apostle Paul did in 2 Corinthians 11:16—12:13.

But the adverb "well" may also mean that you are thanking the Lord in a way that His grace deserves to be treated. Paul often thanked God, not for the obvious blessings, but for the hidden ones for which very few thank God. How the Philippians must have felt when they heard Paul say, "But I would that you should understand, brethren, that the things which happened unto me have fallen out rather unto the furtherance of the gospel" (Phil. 1:12). Paul's principle was, "For none of us [*oudeís*

{3762}, meaning absolutely not a single one] lives to himself, and no man dies to himself" (Rom. 14:7). Not even when we thank the Lord should we be indifferent as to whom of our fellow humans hears us and should be able to join in our thanksgiving and praise. Those who hear us and agree with us that God is praiseworthy will say "Amen," but there are others who will say that we are thanking God for that which most people consider a cause for complaint. Who would thank the Lord for prison chains, as Paul did in Philippians 1:14? "And many of the brethren in the Lord, waxing confident by my bonds, are much more bold to speak the word without fear." There are many saints who thank the Lord for His strengthening them to go through afflictions victoriously, as those in Hebrews 11:33–40, and who are not ashamed to recite their experiences in thanksgiving. This impresses those who are under the wrong idea that deliverance only means rescuing out of oppressive circumstances and not endurance to the end. Physical death may be a part of God's deliverance because it will guarantee the believer a better resurrection (Heb. 11:35).

The prayer of thanksgiving of a child of God should be in an understandable language to encourage other believers. Some may have a different view of life and death, thinking that death is the end of a useful life for the Christian. In reality though, death is the assurance of a better resurrection and a life of liberation from the frailties of the body and earthly difficulties and limitations.

Therefore, the advice of Paul is that our prayers should not be to God only who really does not need to hear our prayers verbalized for He knows our hearts, they should be also for the benefit of our fellow humans to understand the attitude of our hearts.

"Is Not Edified"

The word "not" is the negative *ouk* (3756). This negative tells us that when we speak in an unknown tongue, there is absolutely no way whereby we can contribute to the spiritual growth of the other persons if they cannot understand our reason for thanking the Lord. Verbalization and comprehensibility of our prayers would apply to the edification of both those who are in agreement and disagreement with us. When Stephen was dying for his faith, there was a young man by the name of Saul who witnessed his death. He not only saw Stephen die, but also heard him speak. Saul was fully cognizant of what Stephen was saying as he spoke to the Lord. Stephen's testimony and prayer demonstrated his belief that death was not the end, but rather that it was the deliverance of his spirit into the safekeeping of the Lord Jesus Christ, for he said, "Lord Jesus, receive my spirit" (Acts 7:59).

Stephen's comments further revealed his attitude toward those who were precipitating his death: "Lord, lay not this sin to their charge" (Acts 7:60). He recognized what they were doing as sin, but he was not resentful. He did not want the Lord to count it for their eternal punishment, but to count it forgivable. Certainly this prayer had a profound effect in the life of at least one violent persecutor present by the name of Saul who was later converted as a result of God's blinding light on the road to Damascas and became a heroic defender of the faith. Let not your prayers of thanksgiving be in an unknown tongue, but in that which others can understand and rejoice and praise God with you.

LESSONS:

1. Our prayers of thanksgiving are to be heard by God and fellow believers.

CONSIDERATION OF OTHERS

2. Our prayers of thanksgiving are an acknowledgment that whatever God's grace permits is well received by us.
3. Thus even in weaknesses and adverse circumstances we can thank the Lord.
4. God really does not have to hear our words spoken to know what is in our heart. He knows our very thoughts.
5. To our fellow human beings, whether they agree with us or not, our words are important. Speak them loudly, clearly, and understandably. Others should hear our thanksgiving.

1 Cor. 14:18, 19 | *Reason Must Prevail*

*I thank my God, I speak with tongues more than ye all:
Yet in the church I had rather speak five words with my
understanding, that by my voice I might teach others also,
than ten thousand words in an unknown tongue.*

Paul's Use of Tongues

To many, Paul's declaration that he spoke with tongues more than the Corinthians did is a real puzzle. Up to this point, and again later in the chapter, he condemns the Corinthians who spoke in a mysterious manner. Why does he here thank God that he does the very thing he apparently condemns? The only logical conclusion, as we suggested in past studies, is that Paul is talking about two different ways of speaking with tongues. When Paul mentions the Corinthian practice of speaking with tongues, he means unintelligible utterances not reducible to language forms, originating in the Corinthians' own spirits and emotions. When Paul refers to this, he usually uses the singular form, "speaking in a tongue." In the Greek text, the word "tongue" in its metaphorical meaning, referring to speech and not the physical organ, takes the singular form (vv. 2, 4, 13, 14, 19, 26, and 27). This is justifiably identified in the KJV as "an unknown tongue," despite the fact that the word "unknown" does not occur in the Greek text. It is unknown to linguists; it is not spoken by any language group of people; it cannot be reduced to phonetic syllables.

Dr. William E. Welmers, Professor of African Languages at the University of California at Los Angeles, writes:

> We do know something about representative languages of every known language family in the world. I am by no means unique among descriptive linguists in having had direct, personal contact with well over a hundred languages representing a majority of the world's language families, and in having studied descriptions of languages of virtually every reported type. If a glossolalic (i.e., one who professes to speak in unknown tongues in the Holy Spirit's power) were speaking any of the thousand languages of Africa, there is about a 90 percent probability that I would know it in a minute. Now, I have also had the opportunity of making a sympathetic study of an alleged instance of speaking in tongues. And I must report without reservation that my sample does not sound like a language structurally. . . . The consonants and vowels do not all sound like English (the glossolalic's native language), but the intonation patterns are so completely American English that the total effect is a bit ludicrous. My sample includes an "interpretation." At the most generous estimate, the glossolalic utterance includes ten or eleven "sentences" or stretches of possibly meaningful speech. But the "interpretation" involves no less than fourteen distinct and independent ideas. There simply can be no match between the "tongue" and the "interpretation." I am told that Dr. E. A. Nida of the American Bible Society has reported similar impressions of glossolalic recordings. Our evidence is still admittedly limited, but from the viewpoint of a Christian linguist the modern phenomenon of glossolalia would appear to be a linguistic fraud and monstrosity, given even the most generous interpretation of 1 Corinthians 12—14 [*Christianity Today*, 8 Nov. 1963: 127, 28].

When Paul speaks of his own ability to speak with tongues he does not mean unintelligible utterances but known languages employed to make the grace of God known to men. We must conclude that whenever known intelligible languages are meant, Paul uses the plural form, "tongues," and not "a tongue" (see vv. 5, 6, 18, 21, and 23). Thus, in verse 18, which we are now examining, we find Paul saying, "I thank my God, I speak with tongues more than ye all." By this he means known intelligible languages, native to various groups of people, who can understand them without the use of an interpreter. The Corinthians, who lived in a cosmopolitan center of trade, no doubt had at least a smattering of various languages, but Paul said he spoke more languages than they. He was not implying that he was indiscriminately mouthing these foreign languages as they were doing with their unknown tongue. He could show off his linguistic abilities if he wanted to, but he did not. He simply states in so many words that he could. This verse might very well be paraphrased, "I thank God that I have the ability to speak more real languages than any of you and all of you put together." He was referring to his natural ability to speak various human languages. Paul undoubtedly spoke the language of the day, Aramaic, and acquired an understanding of Hebrew from his study of the Scriptures. That he spoke Greek is evident from Acts 21:37, "And as Paul was to be led into the castle, he said unto the chief captain, May I speak unto thee? Who said, Canst thou speak Greek?" It also seems likely that he spoke Latin, and that he used Latin to convince the chief captain that he was a Roman citizen: "And as they bound him with thongs, Paul said unto the centurion that stood by, Is it lawful for you to scourge a man that is a Roman, and uncondemned? When the centurion heard that, he went and told the chief captain, saying, Take heed what thou doest: for this man is a Roman. Then the chief captain came, and said unto him, Tell me, art thou a Roman? He said, Yea. And the chief captain answered, With a great sum obtained I this freedom. And Paul said, But I was free born" (Acts 22:25–28).

I Had Rather Speak Five Words

Having said that he possessed this ability, Paul goes on in verse 19 to make the practical application of how he would conduct himself at worship in the local assembly of believers at any time in which they might happen to meet for worship. This is indicated by his use of the aorist tense (*lalēsa*, 2980) instead of the present indicative for the verb "speak." "But in the church," he says (and here by "church" he means an assembly of believers and others who might be present), "I want to speak at that particular time of the gathering, whatever time that might be, five words with my understanding," or "reason" or "mind" (i.e., mental power and process, reasoning power and process). By speaking in a foreign language that those present could not understand, or by uttering ecstatic sounds unintelligible to his hearers, he implied he would not be using his mind.

In verse 18 Paul tells what he can do, but in verse 19 he stresses that what one can do is not always the advisable and profitable thing to do. Paul cannot possibly be referring to the unknown tongue of the Corinthians in verse 18 because he certainly would not claim he was able to do something he condemns the Corinthians for doing. Nor does the contrast merely imply that in ecstasy he would speak much, whereas when using his mind he would speak less. The use of the mind does not necessarily involve control of the quantity of words spoken but the quality, and that not the inherent quality of the words themselves but their usefulness to those who hear them. Throughout his argument Paul is more concerned with the hearers than with the speaker. He stresses that it is not so important what good speaking in any language or in an unknown tongue will do to the speaker, but how it will affect the hearers.

Thus in verses 18 and 19 he presents a masterful parallel between his ability to speak in various languages and his selection of the language that he must use. This language must be understood by his hearers, for though it were a known, intelligible language, if it were unknown to his hearers he would be unintelligent to use it. In verse 14 he declares that one who speaks in ecstatic utterances is not using his mind, since he does not understand what he is saying. In verses 18 and 19 he says that one does not use his mind even if he selects an intelligible language that he himself understands but his hearers do not.

That I Might Teach

It is just as though I were to address an American audience in Greek, knowing full well that they do not understand Greek. What difference would it make to them whether I jabbered in Greek or in a so-called unknown tongue, as the Corinthians did? In either case, it would show that I was not using my mind. And what should be the purpose of my speaking even five words? Paul says it is to "teach others." The word for "teach" here is *katēchēsō* (from *katēchéō*, 2727) in Greek, from which we get our word "catechize." *Katēchéō*, which basically means "to resound," also means "to sound a thing in one's ears, to impress it upon one by word of mouth, to instruct by word of mouth."

Observe the word "also" in this clause, "that I might teach others also." I am not to think of myself only but to consider others. I should not consider my own ecstatic spiritual experience the important thing, but whenever I open my mouth in public worship I should consider whether I am benefiting others by what I say. This will help me to get away from the selfish concept of God as one who centers His attention on me and worship Him in the greater context of His concern for others also.

Note that verse 19 begins with the adversative "but" (*allá*, 235), to indicate a contrast between what Paul said he could do in verse 18 and what he could never do in verse 19. "I can speak a number of foreign languages," he says, "but I cannot speak in unintelligible utterances as you do." He never claimed ability to speak in unintelligible utterances. "But suppose I did," he says in verse 19. "Should I use this so-called gift, or refrain for the common good?" To possess abilities is one thing, but if their use is not always in the best interests of the congregation, should we let others suffer that we may satisfy our own egos?

The unselfish Christian, who is often also more mature, will defer his personal satisfaction out of consideration for others. He will refrain from "taking over" in a given situation when a younger Christian needs the experience of praying, testifying, or conducting a meeting. He will restrain himself from expressing his opinions on minor matters before those who are babes in the faith, lest he disturb them with controversy that might cause them to stumble. He will relinquish having his own way if he finds that would be disruptive of the common good. Even so Paul wants these Corinthian Christians to be mature enough to be willing to forego their own spiritual satisfactions in public worship in order to further the spiritual needs of the congregation as a whole.

LESSONS:

1. Paul was thankful to God that he could speak several intelligible languages to people who could understand them without using a translator. The cosmopolitan Corinthian Christians, on the other hand, had only a smattering of a couple of languages. And, their "unknown tongue" was not a language at all.
2. If Paul had wanted to, he could have run linguistic circles around them and made himself understood with real languages.
3. Here Paul was not implying that he too was indiscriminately mouthing these "tongues" as they were with their "unknown tongue."
4. If given the opportunity to speak formally in the assembly, Paul would rather speak just five rational words than 10,000 "words" using an "unknown tongue." Why? Because, at least there would be a particle of sense imparted to the audience instead of thousands of nonsensical syllables. Paul chose quality over quantity.
5. What is more important—how the message will affect the hearers or how good the individual speaker feels?

1 Cor. 14:20 | *Be Mature in Thought and Speech*

Brethren, be not children in understanding: howbeit in malice be ye children, but in understanding be men.

Though Paul differed quite radically with the Corinthians over their understanding of the whole question of speaking with tongues and felt called upon to rebuke and instruct them, observe how lovingly he addresses them. He has just finished telling them that though he spoke more languages than they did, he would not employ them without the use of his intelligence; nor would he employ the ecstatic utterances with which they were confusing babes in Christ and alienating unbelievers. "In understanding be men," he tells them.

In Understanding

The word translated "understanding" is not the word *noús* (3563) used in the previous verses, but *phresín* (5424), "in the mind," denoting here "wits, senses." "Brethren, be not children in the mind," says Paul. To be children in the mind is to act immaturely, as though one's mental development had been arrested in childhood. Two words for "children" are used here: *paidía* (3813), properly "children," and the verb *nēpiázō* (3515) that comes from *nēpioi* (3516) "babies, infants." "Brethren, do not act like children as far as thinking and judging are concerned: but as far as malice is concerned be babes."

Children

Parents understandably dread it when someone gives a drum or other noisemaking toy to a child. The little ones become so enthralled with the volume of sound they are producing that they are lost to all other considerations. Bang, bang, bang they go all day long, whether quiet is necessary or not. They do not care how much noise they make as long as they are enjoying it themselves. Young children can exercise no discretion. That is the kind of childish Christians the Corinthians were. As long as their tongues possessed this exciting and enthralling ability to rattle, why not let them do it full force? Instead of being thoughtless like children, says Paul, it is better to be babes in malice. He says "infants" (the verb *nēpiázete* [3515], from *nḗpioi* [3516], "infants") and not "children" *(paidía,* 3813) now. Babies sleep a great deal, and when they make noise it is not intentional, it is of necessity. Do not be the type of Christian who will do harm to others, even through the sounds you make volitionally. If you could not help yourself, there might be some excuse for this, but actually this is under your control, so do not engage in noise-making that disturbs others. We can have sympathy for a baby crying, but not for a child banging.

Be Ye

The verb *gínesthe* (1096), translated, "be," is actually "become," which here implies continuous growth. When you speak unintelligibly in public, you act as a child. It is time that you begin to go on from the stage where you first began to "be" a Christian and "become" progressively more mature in your Christian experience. The particular application to the Corinthians at this stage of their development was that they should begin to employ their minds in an adult fashion to produce under-standable speech, rather than to childishly indulge in unintelligible prattling. This rebuke is further proof that Paul could not have meant speaking with unknown tongues when he thanked God for his linguistic ability in verse 18.

This whole matter of Christian maturity is strongly in need of emphasis in congregations today. Babes in Christ often show a reluctance to grow up and assume the responsibilities of full-grown men and women in Christ. They want to remain fixed at the level of being spoon-fed, of acting like spoiled children if they do not get their own way, of regarding their own desires and needs as paramount, of thinking of themselves individually as the exclusive center of God's attention. And the result is the same as in Paul's day: new Christians are upset by their behavior and unbelievers are repelled. "Grow up!" says Paul to these Corinthian Christians.

"Our churches are full of monsters, specimens of arrested growth," says Alexander Maclaren, and he goes on to ask some very pointed questions:

> Have you any more of Christ's beauty in your characters, any more of His grace in your hearts, any more of His truth in your minds than you had a year ago, ten years ago, or at that far-off period when some of you first professed to be Christians? Have the years taught you nothing? There are numbers of people who fancy that if they have once exercised faith in Jesus Christ they may safely and sinlessly stand still. . . . The sure way to reduce your knowledge of Jesus Christ is to neglect increasing it and applying it to your daily life. God's Word tells us that the alternative to growth is apostasy. [See Maclaren, Alexander, *The I and II Epistles of Peter.* London: Hodder and Stoughton, 1910: 234ff.]

Being fixed at the level of tongue-speaking, an emotionally induced experience that bypassed the intellect completely, these Corinthians were in danger of neglecting "the best gifts," which

Paul describes as "faith, hope, charity [love]," manifested in behavior that would edify the church.

"But how do I become a mature Christian?" you ask. Just as you cannot grow physically into a strong healthy adult without daily food and exercise, so you cannot become a spiritually strong adult without daily feeding on God's Word, daily exercise in prayer, and daily application of the insights gained as to what God requires of you to the practical problems of life. Feeding on the Word is not just reading so many verses a day, mechanically as a duty, but committing yourself to a program of life-long Bible study, really digesting and assimilating the truths of Scripture. The result will be that they become part of your very character and govern your relationship to God and the world around you. Prayer, too, cannot be indulged in by fits and starts; it is as necessary as the air you breathe, or the daily exercise of your muscles.

What was missing in the Corinthian congregation is missing in so many of our churches today. People expect to grow spiritually without effort, like plants or animals; but the mind, the will, the whole person are involved in our spiritual development and must be involved wholeheartedly with the Spirit of God in order that we may reach "the measure of the stature of the fullness of Christ" (Eph. 4:13).

LESSONS:

1. Paul was telling them not to think like children, as if their powers of judgment were suspended.
2. Paul was appealing to their mature instincts. They had it in their power to control their glossolalic behavior.
3. Paul counseled them to begin employing their minds in an adult manner to produce understandable speech instead of childish gibberish.
4. Like vomiting (normally an involuntary action), with effort glossolalia can also be self-induced. Both are disgusting.

BE MATURE IN THOUGHT AND SPEECH

1 Cor. 14:21 | *Predicted Long Ago*

In the law it is written, With men of other tongues and other lips will I speak unto this people; and yet for all that will they not hear me, saith the Lord.

Tongues: A Special Witness to the Jews

We have discovered two things thus far regarding this matter of speaking in tongues. First, on the three occasions in Acts of the Apostles when we find the Jews, the Gentiles, and the disciples of John speaking in tongues, they spoke foreign languages known to their hearers. Their words were immediately understood without the necessity of interpretation. The purpose of their speaking in tongues was to make the message of God known to others, especially at Pentecost, and in the case of Caesarea and Ephesus to demonstrate that the Holy Spirit is not a monopoly of the Jews but is also for the Gentiles (Caesarea) and the disciples of John the Baptist (Ephesus). Their communication was from men to men and not from men to God. In all likelihood, these foreign languages had not been acquired in the natural process of learning but were given to them temporarily through the special enablement of the Holy Spirit. This is basically what was involved in the three historical instances of speaking in tongues in the Acts. The record is there to be examined.

Second, we have seen that the way the Corinthians spoke in an unknown tongue was quite different from these historical instances. Their practice involved ejaculating in non-linguistic sounds when in an ecstatic emotional state—sounds that could not be immediately understood by the hearers but had to be interpreted if this were at all possible. Paul implied that interpretation would make the Corinthian practice less objectionable to himself and less damaging to new converts and unbelievers. Later, in verse 28, he tells them that if their speech is not interpretable, they should remain silent.

Other Tongues

Now, in 1 Corinthians 14:21, he cites a prophecy in Isaiah 28:11, 12 to show that the primary reason God enabled His people to speak in languages other than their own was for a witness to the unbelieving Jews.

The main reason Paul refers to this prophecy from Isaiah is to illustrate from the history of the Jewish people how God's dealing with them in a particular instance is symbolic of His overall dealing with the Corinthians. "In the law [that is, the Old Testament] it is written that in alien or other languages, and through alien lips I will speak to this people, and not even then will they listen to me, said the Lord" (a.t.). In order to understand this, we must take it as an illustration of the conclusion Paul is coming to in the next verse, which he introduces with the word *hŏste* (5620), "therefore" or "wherefore."

Although this prophecy was written within the context of the Assyrian captivity of the Northern Kingdom of Israel and the unsuccessful invasion of Judah by Assyria, it had its Messianic fulfillment at Pentecost, when the Lord spoke to the Jewish people assembled, through the extraordinary dispatching of the Holy Spirit. They were from "every nation under heaven." Jews of the Dispersion may have acquired a smattering of Aramaic (Hebrew dialect) but whose native tongue was the language of the land where they had been born (Acts 2:8). At Pentecost the Jews truly were spoken to by the Lord in alien languages (*en* [1722] *heteroglōssois* [2084]). It is noteworthy that the Greek word translated "in other tongues" in 1 Corinthians 14:21 has the meaning of "other than your own yet retaining the basic characteristic of language," as we saw in our examination of Acts 2:4. Thus, looking back, we can truly say that the Jews as a nation (Acts 2:14) and as individuals were witnessed to in languages other than their own Hebrew tongue, through the apostles, by divine enablement.

This was the case at Pentecost (the most striking occasion of speaking in tongues), where we find Jewish Christians speaking to the unbelieving Jews (many of whom were from foreign parts) not only in Hebrew but in foreign languages that the witnessing disciples had never learned, in order that every one of the Jews from these many places might clearly hear the gospel in the language that he personally understood. Although at Caesarea and Ephesus, where the other two instances of speaking with tongues took place, those who spoke were in one case Gentiles, the hearers also included Jews, although in these two cases the Jews were believers. Let us not lose sight of the fact that at Pentecost primarily we have the initial manifestation of the Holy Spirit to the Jews as a group, and it is this predominantly that constitutes the fulfillment of the prophecy of Isaiah. In the instance of Caesarea, it is evident that the main purpose of speaking in tongues was not for the sake of the hearers, who were already believing Jews, but for the sake of the speakers, to persuade them that "on the Gentiles also was poured out the gift of the Holy Ghost." This was proof indisputable that the Holy Spirit, being God, is no respecter of persons. And in Ephesus the same principle is stressed concerning the coming of the Holy

Spirit upon the disciples of John the Baptist, who are said to stand as a bridge between the Old and the New Testaments.

Nevertheless, the Jews were and are known as God's chosen ones. Time and time again He calls them His people. He had, has, and will have very special dealings with them. He wants them to believe. He allowed the first witness to be given to them. He will not give them up to the very end.

It is this witness to the Jews that Paul stresses as he refers to the prophecy from Isaiah. He says in 1 Corinthians 14:21, "In the law it is written, With men of other tongues and other lips will I speak unto this people." This prophecy is taken out of a passage that deals with the time when Judah was unsuccessfully invaded by the Assyrians under Sennacherib. There is no doubt that the expression "this people" meant the Jews. That is what the Lord meant when He spoke through Isaiah, and that is what Paul meant when he referred to speaking with foreign languages.

The historical account in 2 Kings chapter eighteen tells us that Sennacherib the Assyrian had attempted to terrify the Jews who were defending the wall of Jerusalem. He wanted Judah to understand just what would happen to them if they continued to resist. His messengers began to speak in Hebrew so that all the Jews would hear their threats. But the Jewish diplomats begged them not to because they did not want their own people to understand them and lose heart. "Speak, I pray thee, to thy servants in the Syrian language," they said, "for we understand it: and talk not with us in the Jews' language in the ears of the people that are on the wall" (2 Kgs. 18:26). This was a request that the Jews be spoken to in a foreign language. It was a known language but foreign to the Jews. So were the languages spoken at Pentecost, Caesarea, and Ephesus. This is what Paul brings out—that in every historical instance it was known foreign languages that were spoken and not unknown tongues as practiced at Corinth.

The Assyrians, however, contemptuously ignored the Jews' request to speak in Syrian and spoke in Hebrew. In 2 Kings 18:28 we read, "Then Rabshakeh stood and cried with a loud voice in the Jews' language." This one incident was the marked exception to the general but only partial fulfillment of Isaiah's prophecy in the history of Judah at the time of its invasion by the Assyrians, and when the northern ten tribes were carried into captivity by Assyria. The Assyrians were men of a tongue strange to the Jews. The complete fulfillment of this prophecy took place particularly and preeminently at Pentecost, when the Jews were spoken to not only in Hebrew but in languages other than their own. The point Paul is making is that the Corinthian practice of speaking in an unknown tongue had nothing to do with this prophecy or with the historical occurrences of speaking in foreign languages.

This chapter is sealed. Paul seems to say to the Corinthians that God has already fulfilled this prophecy. The Jews have already had this witness of being fought against constantly by foreigners and of being spoken to in other ways, among them in other (unlearned) languages by the apostles, so that they would fully understand what was being said to them, and if the witness heard was not unto conviction of sin and repentance it would be unto judgment (Matt. 11:20–24; 13:11ff; Mark 4:12; Luke 8:10). If they could not understand the language spoken, however, they could not be held responsible. Understanding the message of God places the responsibility squarely on the hearer as to whether he will accept or reject it.

Paul continues telling the Corinthians. "Do not try to say that your speaking in tongues unknown to you and others is the fulfillment of the promise in Isaiah 28:11, 12 or the one in Mark 16:17." As we have seen previously, this latter promise refers not to those who would believe later, like the Corinthians, but to those who had already believed when Christ gave it, that is, the disciples.

Tongues: Right Motive, Wrong Method

The Apostle Paul quoted a prophecy from Isaiah 28:11, 12 to prove that it was God's purpose to speak "with men of other tongues" as a special witness to the Jews. Paul was drawing a parallel between the disobedience of the nations of Judah and the Northern Kingdom of Israel to God in Isaiah's day, and the disobedience of the Jews of Paul's day to God.

The Hebrews' disobedience to God during Isaiah's day resulted in the successful Assyrian capture of the Northern Kingdom of Israel and their unsuccessful capture of Judah. This was a witness of promise and of judgment. The promise was not merely that God would speak to the Hebrews through "men of other tongues," that is, in foreign languages as He did at Pentecost and elsewhere, but the second part of this prophecy says in effect through "men of . . . other lips," that is, Gentile lips. We find no fulfillment of this prophecy in the history of the Hebrews as a people unless we consider the unsuccessful invasion of Judah under the Assyrians as such, even though it was not the Lord Himself who spoke directly to the Hebrews at that time, though He did speak to the Hebrews indirectly through the providential events of the Assyrian captivity of the Northern Kingdom and through the Assyrians' threat to the kingdom of Judah. And in New Testament times, Luke was the only non-Hebrew among the evangelists, and there is no evidence that he did much preaching to the Jews.

Where, then, shall we seek for the fulfillment of the second part of this prophecy? In particular, three times—at Pentecost, at Caesarea, and at Ephesus—the Jews received a witness in languages other than their own, under the direct influence of the Holy Spirit. This does not mean, of course, that they were not witnessed to in their own language. In fact, most of this witnessing was in Aramaic, a Hebrew dialect. This was the language in which the Lord Jesus and the apostles preached. But it pleased the Lord to give the Jews a special sign, a witness in foreign languages that those who spoke to them did not previously know. (See 1 Cor. 14:22.) The Holy Spirit came upon His witnesses to enable them to speak in foreign languages to the Jews, on particular occasions only, for a sign. When they rejected God's extraordinary and special witness to them as a nation, He did not cease His witness. He continues it through the lips of aliens, that is, Gentiles. This prophecy is being fulfilled to this very day, in a broader sense.

"And yet for all that will they not hear me, saith the Lord." What grief this must occasion Him, to be rejected by a people and nation He had so favored. During this present age, His Spirit witnesses to them predominantly through the lips of Gentiles. This is as it ought to be. All of us ought to pray for the peace of Jerusalem.

Nearly every major American city inhabited by a large number of Jews has a Hebrew mission society. Some of these are staffed by Jewish Christians, but the greatest number of preachers and witnesses to the Jews are Gentile Christians. These witnesses do not usually employ the Hebrew language but they speak in their non-Hebrew native languages, in English, German, Russian, and so forth, as necessity directs. The important phrase here is "as necessity directs"; that is, when the hearers do not understand the speaker's native language, or for a special sign, as at Pentecost. The general rule, however, that God has established and in which the Apostle Paul concurs is that men should speak so that others can understand them. If men cannot speak a language that others can understand, the Holy Spirit can enable them to speak it without having learned it. This He did three times that we know of during the apostolic age, and perhaps at other times in the case of individual witness to His people throughout the world. If, however, the element of understandability is missing, if no one in the audience can understand it, the claim that one is speaking in tongues is not genuine.

Only a small minority of Jews today know Hebrew as well as the languages of the lands where they were born and reared during the long years of their dispersion. Although the modern state of Israel is reversing this trend, the percentage of Hebrews who live there is small compared to their total number. An interesting bit of information on this question of languages is contained in an Associated Press Dispatch of July 29, 1963, regarding newspapers published in Israel. "The tiny fifteen-year-old state only has a population of about 2.25 million, but it has twenty-five daily newspapers, sixty weeklies, 140 fortnightlies and monthlies. The dailies are printed in Hebrew, German, Arabic, Hungarian, French, Yiddish, Romanian, English and Bulgarian." [As of September, 1997 the Israel Ministry of Foreign Affairs estimates the population at 5.8 million, eighty-one percent being Jewish.] What hinders us from concluding that the Apostle Paul referred to Isaiah's prophecy as being fulfilled also in a more general way in this age?

Unfortunately, though the Jews have received a consistent Christian witness since apostolic times, they have not as a nation heard the voice of God to repent and accept the Lord Jesus as their Messiah. "They will not hear me, in spite of all I have done for them," God says in effect. The word translated "hear" in Greek is *eisakoúsontai* (1522), which includes obedience as well as hearing. The Jews are hearing a great deal about the Messiah today, and we should continue witnessing to them, but most of them will not obey.

Through the use of this Old Testament passage about speaking in tongues, Paul wants the Corinthians to understand that their practice of speaking with tongues, spectacular as it might seem, could not induce belief in Christ. No doubt the Corinthians sincerely thought that their unknown tongues would so impress people as to attract them to the Lord, insofar as this was their motive, it was commendable. Paul recognized this, which is why he did not scold them more openly but sought to reason with them about their method. It is as if he were saying to them. "My brethren, your speaking with tongues is basically different from the historic and genuine witness of the apostles, which was brought about by God Himself. Even so, the Jews did not respond to the Lord. Now you are trying to imitate the work of God. Do you think unbelievers will not recognize this as unreal, a fake? They are the ones you have in mind, perhaps, but they will think you are out of your mind when you speak to them in a language (if it can be called that) that they cannot understand" (a.t.). That is the gist of Paul's argument to the Corinthians. Their motive may have been good, but their method was not in that they were trying to revive something the Holy Spirit had only employed three times and were trying to do so through their own spirits, not His. One wonders whether the frequency with which the Corinthians were speaking in tongues was not an added evidence of its being merely imitative of the true experience.

LESSONS:

1. In the Book of Acts, the communicative events were between people, not from human beings to God. Therefore, God chose to use natural languages as the normal means of communication but to empower people to do so supernaturally for a brief time, without the necessity of their spending many years to acquire this linguistic ability.
2. What the Corinthian Christians were doing was quite different from what took place in Acts. They were erratically spewing forth a linguistic sounds while in a trance-like state of mind. This was causing chaos in the assembly.

PREDICTED LONG AGO

3. The prophecy of Isaiah 28:11, 12 dealt with God's objective of reaching unbelieving Jews through convincing proofs of natural language. This happened on the day of Pentecost in 30 A.D. (Acts 2).
4. Paul is telling the Corinthians that their foolish jabbering was certainly not a fulfillment of the ancient prophet's words.

1 Cor. 14:22 | *Proof*

Wherefore tongues are for a sign, not to them that believe,
but to them that believe not: but prophesying serveth not
for them that believe not, but for them which believe.

Would Miracles Convince the Unbelieving?

Paul presents his arguments in masterly fashion, reasoning logically from cause to effect. He has shown the Corinthians that although the Jews received a miraculous witness through the apostles and early believers who spoke languages they had not learned, they still did not heed the Spirit nor obey His voice. "Now," says Paul to the Corinthians, "here you are speaking in an unintelligible manner with the hope of impressing unbelievers with the gospel. This is futile. Where do you find anywhere in Scripture that the gospel must be preached in unknown and mysterious languages to be persuasive? Nowhere. Why do you do it, then? God used it as a sign to the Jews in particular and they did not heed. That was real speaking with tongues [known foreign languages], and they were not persuaded to follow the Messiah. Do you then think you are going to accomplish it with your unintelligible ecstatic utterances?" (a.t.).

From this emerges a basic and God-given principle, that just as God uses the ordinary means that He has created before

He resorts to extraordinary manifestations of His power and ability, so should we. God has given us the earth and has so constituted the laws of His creation that when we put a seed into the ground under proper conditions it will grow and provide food for our sustenance. He expects us to plow and plant and reap to secure our daily bread, rather than to expect Him to drop manna down from heaven. Yet He is one and the same God who ordains the ordinary processes and performs the extraordinary. The earth could not bear fruit unless He enabled it to do so. The Israelites could not have been fed with manna in the wilderness unless His hand provided it. But why should one seem greater to us than the other? We marvel at the virgin birth of the Lord Jesus; it is right that we should. But let us not cease to wonder at the natural birth of every child, for in the final analysis it is God who makes this possible.

That is why Paul stresses through his arguments in this fourteenth chapter of 1 Corinthians that we are to dedicate ourselves first and foremost to the preaching of the gospel in an orderly and understandable fashion. We are not, of course, to depend primarily on the actual preaching to save souls, but on the Holy Spirit, who is the only One who can energize and utilize the preaching to convict sinners. For the same reason, we cannot place undue value upon any ecstatic experience to which we may expose unbelievers.

There are some people today who say, "If the Lord Jesus Christ were here on earth, and we could see Him with our own eyes after His resurrection from the dead and witness some of the tremendous miracles of which we read in the New Testament, we would believe in Him." And yet many miracles took place during the course of His ministry, and many did not believe. Note the relatively small number of people that the Scriptures tell us assembled to see the Lord in Galilee after His resurrection (Matt. 28:16 and 1 Cor. 15:6).

Paul's first conclusion, then, is that "tongues are for a sign, not to them that believe, but to them that believe not." He is not referring to the unknown tongues of the Corinthians but to real languages as spoken at Pentecost, Caesarea, and Ephesus. Understanding this, the translators of the King James Version did not say "unknown tongues." Paul wants the Corinthians to realize that when God gives His witnesses the ability to speak in foreign languages that they have not learned naturally, as He did on these three historic occasions, He does it not for the sake of persuading believers but to lead unbelievers to the Lord Jesus Christ.

For a Sign

Such languages are given for "a sign," the Apostle says. The Greek word for "sign," *sēmeíon* (4592), is used to denote a miracle also. Among all the names that the miracles bear in the New Testament, their ethical end and purpose comes out in the word *sēmeíon*, "sign," with the most distinctness (see Trench, R. C., *Synonyms of the New Testament*, p. 342). The ability to speak in foreign languages you have never learned is a miracle, says Paul, but it is not a purposeless miracle; it has a goal, and that is the salvation of unbelievers.

For the believers in the audience, speaking with tongues the miracle-working power of God and the gospel. They have experienced it already in their own salvation. They need no sign. As Trench says further about *sēmeíon* (4592), "sign": "It is involved and declared in the very word that the prime object and end of the miracle is to lead us to something out of and beyond itself: that, so to speak, it is a kind of finger-post of God, pointing for us to this: valuable, not so much for what it is, as for what it indicates of the grace and power of the doer, or of his immediate connection with a higher spiritual world" (Trench, pp. 342, 343). Since, then, those that believe have already been pointed to God, says Paul, there is no need for miraculous speaking in foreign languages, let alone the imitation of it that exists among you.

For Them That Believe Not

It is interesting to note that the expression "them that believe" in the Greek text is a present participle. It is "the believing ones." This is immediately followed by the adjectival form of the verb "believe not." This should not be translated "them that believe not" but "the unbelievers." The present active participle "the believing ones" connotes a condition in the process of formation, those who are in the process of believing or those who have already or may have just believed. It emphasizes more the inception, the beginning of belief than the permanent state of believing, which of course is implied also. The verse should more correctly read: "Therefore the languages [foreign languages spoken as a result of the enablement of the Holy Spirit and not learned—for if they were learned they could not be considered a sign or miracle] are for a sign, not to the believing ones but to the unbelievers." It is as if Paul were telling the Corinthians that those who have believed or are in the process of believing do not need any outward sign or miracle such as took place at Pentecost. The Spirit of God had already worked in their hearts. It is the confirmed unbelievers who demand a sign. But even if it were given them they would not believe. So why all this fuss about speaking in tongues, which in the three instances recorded in the Acts of the apostles was a real miracle, but in your case is not?

Paul's second conclusion in verse 22 is, "But prophesying serveth not for them that believe not, but for them which believe." Here prophesying means teaching, declaring God's Word, the regular ministry of the proclamation of the gospel as contrasted to the miraculous speaking with tongues. Believers need to be taught all that God has already revealed, and solidly established in the faith. Therefore, among them we are to practice prophesying, which has always been done in the common language of the people. In this last part of the verse, the same Greek forms of the verb "believe" are used. When Paul refers to "unbelievers," the adjective *apístois* (571) is used, and when he refers to the believers it is the present participial form, *toís* (3588) *pisteúousin* (4100), "the believing ones."

Although Paul spoke in verse 21 of the Jews receiving a witness through foreign languages known to them, the application in verse 22 need not be limited to the Jews. In this age of grace, as far as our salvation goes, there is no distinction between Jews and Gentiles; we are either believers or unbelievers, regardless of our church affiliations. That is the only distinction God makes in His Word. Let us not make much of other artificial distinctions.

LESSONS:

1. It is futile to think that unbelievers would be impressed by the speaking of an unintelligible tongue.
2. The ability to preach the gospel in a foreign language that one has never studied was astonishing to the unconverted who heard it (Acts 2:4–11; 10:46; 19:6). They regarded it as a proof from God that the gospel message was authentic.
3. The proper target for teaching God's Word (prophesying) are believers. This is to be done in the common language of the people, not with glossolalia.

1 Cor. 14:23 | *Insanity?*

If therefore the whole church be come together into one place, and all speak with tongues, and there come in those that are unlearned, or unbelievers, will they not say that ye are mad?

How to Behave in the Assembly

So far in our study of Paul's teaching on the subject of speaking in tongues, we have seen that he made a distinction between the known foreign languages in which the Holy Spirit enabled the disciples and others to speak at Pentecost, Ephesus, and Caesarea, and the unintelligible, mysterious, ecstatic utterances of the Corinthian believers. He indicated that speaking in tongues should be permitted only if those present could understand what was being said (either directly or through an interpreter), and condemned unintelligible utterances as detrimental to the unbeliever or the babe in Christ who might attend the local assembly of believers. He made a strong plea for Christian maturity in this matter, for other-centeredness rather than self-centeredness in public worship.

Paul's main concern as he writes to the Corinthian believers is what impression their Christian worship will make on visitors to the congregation who are searching for the truth for their own lives. This should concern us, too. In the enjoyment of our Christian experiences, whether individually or collectively, we must never forget that the eyes of the world are upon us. We must not, of course, accommodate ourselves, especially in our behavior, to the expectations of the world, or water down the truth to please them, but we must never forget the purpose for which we are in the world: to glorify God and proclaim His truth to others. Paul says we cannot do this if we speak unintelligibly.

If

Again, to make the admonition gentler, Paul suggests a hypothetical case. "Let us suppose you have a meeting of the whole congregation in one place and all are speaking in tongues," he says in effect. A hypothesis, such as this, often has its root in fact, and there is little doubt that the Corinthians often did hold meetings such as this. But Paul does not level an accusation at them. He says, "If."

When I want to correct my son for some wrongdoing, I do not usually accuse him directly of his misbehavior, instead I speak hypothetically, asking him what he would think of someone else who had performed a similar act. In this way he is led to judge the wrongness of his action without being put on the defensive and is much more likely to acknowledge that a change of conduct is in order. This seems to be Paul's method in the entire fourteenth chapter of 1 Corinthians as he lovingly seeks to correct the abuses and misconceptions that have sprung up in connection with speaking with tongues. There is room to believe that he was highly successful because he evidently did not find it necessary to mention this matter at all in his second epistle to them. If the abuses had continued, would he not have spoken about them again, after having given them a prominent place in his first letter?

INSANITY?

What can we learn from the Apostle Paul in correcting our erring brethren? Where possible, avoid bluntness and use the hypothetical method. Seek to make the other person realize his own error without pointing it out yourself. Make generous use of the word "suppose" when mentioning a fault.

The Whole Church

What is meant by "the church (*ekklēsía*, 1577)" here? It is obviously not a building but the members of the local assembly of believers. We do well to remember the real meaning of the term "church"—not a lifeless building but living people who desire to worship the Lord. They can do this no matter where they meet. Here in Corinth it may have been a home or any public meeting place. No mention is made of it because it is not significant. What is significant is that Christians gathered together for collective worship. We may "attend church" for a variety of reasons: because we feel it is our duty, because others expect it of us, because we would feel guilty if we did not, because it makes us look upright and moral in the eyes of the community, because we want to meet our friends there. But how many of us actually meet together with our fellow believers for the conscious purpose of collective worship?

A Hindu student from India attended the morning worship service at one of the leading evangelical churches of California. He was much impressed with the beautiful building, saying that it was "much finer than our temples in India." But he was astonished to learn that it was used mainly on Sunday mornings, with a much smaller Sunday evening congregation and only a handful turning up for the midweek prayer meeting. "Do you mean to tell me that you have this elaborate, expensive building for use only two or three times a week?" he asked. "In India we go to prayer in our Hindu temples every morning at sunrise and every night at sunset. The Muslims go to prayer five times daily. How can you expect us to accept Christianity when we pray more to our gods than you do to yours?" Sometimes it would appear that, we are more concerned with a program of building splendid church edifices than with engaging in a fellowship of living creatures for the purpose of worshiping and serving the almighty God.

This passage illustrates the custom of the local believers of meeting in one appointed place for public worship. "If . . . the whole church be come together into one place," says Paul. This specific mention of an occasion on which the whole congregation met suggests that there might have been other meetings attended by fewer members of the local congregation for fellowship of one believer with another, such as might be found in our churches today: prayer meetings, testimony meetings, women's missionary society meetings, and so forth. Unbelievers seldom attend such meetings. But Paul is concerned with the general meetings which were open to the public. They must not provide a basis for causing a prejudice against the gospel.

We are not justified in assuming that this hypothetical case put forth by Paul is purely suppositional. It is obvious from the context that it had its basis in fact and was only stated hypothetically for the sake of diplomacy. Paul's writings abound in hypothetical cases. The fifteenth chapter of 1 Corinthians is full of them. Paul constantly seeks to impress upon the Corinthians the importance of the resurrection of the Lord Jesus Christ by supposing what the consequences would be if it had not taken place. "If Christ be not raised," he says, "your faith is vain; ye are yet in your sins" (v. 17). He invites them to envision the awful consequences of something that is not in fact true, in order that they may properly appreciate the blessings that are theirs because of what is true. And here in 1 Corinthians 14:23, he invites them to envision the dire consequences of speaking in unknown tongues in a public worship service (something which undoubtedly was true, but which he tactfully states as a mere supposition), in order that the Corinthians may be led to see the error of their ways for themselves.

Babbling or Blessing?

Although Paul well knew that the Corinthian believers were holding meetings at which many persons were speaking in unknown tongues at the same time, to the confusion of many in the worship service, he gently suggests that if such a thing did occur it might give rise to grave doubts as to their sanity. Some less understanding and loving persons might have come right out and accused them of acting like lunatics; but Paul wants to win them, not antagonize them.

Paul tactfully excludes the possibility that this refers to all the believers gathered together at this public meeting, all speaking at the same time, thus creating an atmosphere of bedlam, although this was really what was taking place. We may gather from what Paul tactfully states that if this were so, that is, if all spoke together, it would then have made no difference whether the tongues spoken were ecstatic utterances or known foreign languages, the effect would have been the same. I know what confusion can result when all four of my children used to clamor for my attention at once. Imagine then a group of a hundred or more people speaking all at once, even if it were in English, and the effect would be that of a madhouse. People do not have to speak in unknown tongues to create this atmosphere of confusion and madness. Here the Apostle refers to each one in the group speaking in his turn. Whether a great many people speak together in their own language, loudly and all at once, or whether each speaks in turn a language not commonly understood, the result is confusion. Paul is concerned not so much with how we worship God but with what effect our public worship will have on others.

And All Speak with Tongues

What is the actual meaning of "tongues" here? Since the plural form is used, it probably means foreign languages. The King James Version does not use the word "unknown" before "tongues" in this instance. What would be the meaning of this verse if we were to take "tongues" here to mean languages? Up until now we have seen that whenever the plural form of the word is used we could take it to mean known human languages. We can do the same thing here with perfect consistency if we recall that this group of believers in Corinth was a cosmopolitan one, familiar with a variety of languages. Such knowledge can be a good thing; Paul has no quarrel with them on that score. In verse 18 he speaks thankfully of knowing many languages, and in verse 5 he says, "I would that ye all spake in tongues [languages]." But we must be selective in the languages we use, taking into consideration what our hearers can understand. A person of good judgment and sound mind will choose a language known to his hearers. On the day of Pentecost, the Holy Spirit gave the apostles the ability to speak in languages that the people understood. Paul is not dealing here with what is actually spoken; he is concerned with things spoken but not understood.

The Corinthians had the all-too-human characteristic of showing off their accomplishments. Could it be that they liked to exhibit their ability to speak in languages other than their own? Perhaps they even thought that any strangers present could be evangelized in this way. Thus each one who knew one or more foreign languages might get up and speak. Perhaps very few persons might understand them, but the great majority would not. This sort of thing could be repeated over and over, without any semblance of orderliness in the meeting. How much more disorderly and confused would it be if these tongues were non-human, unknown, ecstatic utterances! The strength of

Paul's argument is that, if it is so objectionable to unbelievers to hear you speaking in real languages that only a few in the church can understand, how much more objectionable it must be for them to hear you speaking in ecstatic utterances.

I do not think this is stretching the point. Recall the scene at Pentecost. There the apostles spoke in languages known and understood by their unbelieving hearers, languages which the speakers themselves had not learned but were supernaturally enabled to speak. We do not believe this resulted in confusion because those who heard them immediately understood what was being said. Why, then, did some observers get the impression that the disciples were drunk (Acts 2:13)? It was because the languages they happened to hear were incomprehensible to them. Those who could not understand what the disciples said were scandalized; those who could were amazed.

Whether real languages, foreign to the speakers but native to some hearers, or ecstatic utterances are being spoken is really immaterial because in either case what constitutes the offense is that the majority of hearers cannot understand what is being said. What difference does it make what the speaker says, or what language he speaks, human or non-human, if you cannot understand it? If he continues to jabber away at you, you are likely to conclude that he is out of his mind. This is what Paul emphasized in verse 11 and re-emphasizes here. He is criticizing the person who speaks with a disregard for his hearers, whether they be many or few.

I have often been in the company of polyglots in Europe, and frankly it can be very disconcerting to listen to them compete with one another to see who knows the most languages. They rattle off sentences in one language after another, though very few of their hearers can comprehend them, like little children vying for the spotlight in "show and tell" at school. There is more than a suggestion that this may have been the underlying motive of the Corinthians also. When you disregard your audience, whether by speaking in languages foreign to them or in ecstatic utterances, your hearers will conclude that you are out of your mind.

Remember the basic principle underlying Paul's whole argument. When you speak, do not do it to show how much you know but to try to be of help to others. This is where 1 Corinthians chapter thirteen fits into the context; it is Paul's treatise on love, which "seeketh not her own." The fourteenth chapter is the logical and practical application of Christian love.

If there were those who mocked at the manifestation of the Holy Spirit at Pentecost, how much more will people be inclined to ridicule if the motivation and initiative are not of the Spirit but of self! At Pentecost God wanted each man to hear the gospel in his own language; that was the important thing. But some who could not understand the languages spoken were inclined to mock. Paul supposes a parallel situation in 1 Corinthians 14:23. You remember that in verse 21 he said that in spite of the foreign languages through which God spoke to His people, the Jews, they did not obey Him. Now Paul turns to the Corinthians and says, "Do not think that the unbelievers, whether Jews or Gentiles, will listen to you either when you speak in languages foreign to them or in ecstatic utterances." Underneath it all Paul knew that they had the selfish desire to show off.

Does Our Behavior Repel or Attract?

It is apparent from this verse that unbelievers and those not well-versed in the faith attended the worship services at Corinth. Whether out of curiosity or from a sense of spiritual need, we find that such people also attend our church services today. We must give thought to the effect of the gospel and our behavior in public worship upon them, being careful to attract rather than to repel them. This apparently was not the case in Corinth.

Unlearned or Unbelievers

". . . and [if] there come in those that are unlearned, or unbe-lievers. . . ." The word translated "unlearned" here and in verse sixteen is the Greek noun *idiōtai* (2399), presumably meaning the person who is ignorant or ill-informed in the faith, though not necessarily an uneducated person in other areas. The word translated "unbelievers" is *ápistoi* (571), which refers here, as in verse 22, to a rather confirmed state of unbelief.

"Suppose," says Paul in effect, "that a number of such pagans drop into your services. As they listen to you making sounds which they cannot understand, will they not think you are crazy?" (a.t.). This is the crux of Paul's argument, the lack of un-derstanding that would result, whether the church members speak in foreign languages unknown to most of their hearers or in ecstatic tongues. Note that Paul makes no mention of inter-pretation. "Will they not say that ye are mad?" he asks. Though at Pentecost some mocked, saying that the disciples were drunk, those for whom the languages were intended understood them, and there was general amazement at this phenomenon (see Acts 2:12, 13).

Of course, no matter who speaks or how intelligently he pre-sents the gospel, some people will always mock. But this is be-cause of their hardness of heart and not because of any childish or foolish behavior by the speaker. Some will also believe. "For the preaching of the cross is to them that perish foolishness; but unto us which are saved it is the power of God" (1 Cor. 1:18). This is exactly what happened when Paul preached to the Athen-ian philosophers. "And when they heard of the resurrection of the dead, some mocked: and others said, We will hear thee again of this matter. Howbeit certain men cleaved unto him, and believed" (Acts 17:32, 34).

Observe, however, that there is no mention of anyone believing as a result of this type of meeting in Corinth. In such meetings, where the listeners cannot understand what is being said, Paul sees no possibility of the conviction of the Holy Spirit coming upon the hearts of unbelievers. "Will they not say that ye are mad?" The Greek word translated "ye are mad" in this verse is *maínesthe*. It is the second person plural indicative of the verb *maínomai* (3105), which means "to be mad, to rave, being out of one's mind." This does not refer to permanent insanity but to a temporary state of aberration in one who may be overcome by enthusiasm, or a desire to show off, against his better judgment.

What Paul is actually describing here is a state in which self or the emotions take over and the individual loses control over them with his rational mind. In this particular instance he refers to speaking in languages that cannot be understood by all or most of the hearers, so that the speaker gives the impression of being out of his mind.

Ye Are Mad

The word *maínesthe* (3105) comes from the same Greek root as the English words "mania" or "maniac." Such unreasonable conduct was usually attributed by the ancient Greeks to the activity of demons. In the tenth chapter of John (vv. 17–20), the Lord Jesus made the claim that no one could take His life from Him, that He alone had the power to lay it down. Many of the Jews upon hearing this said, "He hath a devil, and is mad." The expression "and is mad" is the same Greek word *maínetai*.

Observe that the Jews, too, attributed mania to the activity of the devil or demons. In the ancient world demons were often identified with the worships of the heathen. To the pagans *daimónia* (1140) were merely "inferior" divinities and not necessarily bad. Of course, in the New Testament the word refers to evil spirits. Sometimes in Classical Greek *daimónion* refers to the deity, divinity, or divine operation. In Herodotus IV:79 we read, "*hupó* (5259) *toú* (3588) *theoú* (2316) *maínetai* (3105)," meaning "He is acting mad through the activity of the worship," that is, a particular divinity, perhaps. This leads us to conclude that when these Corinthians spoke in tongues in public worship, whether in foreign languages known to only a few of the hearers, or in ecstatic utterances, they were in such a self-centered, emotional state of frenzy that they gave the impression to new believers and unbelievers that they were possessed by demons, or that some outside force, either satanic or divine, was acting upon them in such a way as to render their mental powers inactive.

This is what the Apostle Paul wants to correct. He is opposed to the Corinthians behaving in public worship in such a way as to give outsiders or new believers the idea that God or demons have nullified their natural intelligence. God has given us our minds in order to use them, even in the exercise of our religious duties and in our religious experiences. We must remember the general principle that Paul has been underlining throughout 1 Corinthians chapters thirteen and fourteen, that public worship is not only for the individual's own spiritual benefit but for the edification of the whole body of believers assembled together, and for attracting unbelievers to the Lord Jesus Christ.

LESSONS:

1. In order to soften the blow, Paul suggests a hypothetical situation to the Corinthians, even though it was probably factual.
2. The Greek word *ekklēsía* (1577) is used here. This is one of the clearest instances to show that the meaning of the word denotes a group of people, that is, a local assembly of believers. The English word "church" is a poor translation. Unfortunately, to most people, "church" has the con-

notation of a church building. Christian church buildings did not exist until the third century after Christ.

3. This verse may infer that there were other small gatherings of Christians at different times in Corinth besides the central meeting.

4. If some non-Christian visitors in Corinth were to witness the general confusion of simultaneous tongue-speaking, Paul asks, would they not say that you are crazy?

1 Cor. 14:24, 25 — *Conviction*

But if all prophesy, and there come in one that believeth not, or one unlearned, he is convinced of all, he is judged of all: And thus are the secrets of his heart made manifest; and so falling down on his face he will worship God, and report that God is in you of a truth.

Tongues versus Prophesying

The whole framework of Paul's discussion on speaking with tongues is the worship service of the local church. First Corinthians 14:24 assumes the same setting as verse 23, that is, the whole body of Corinthian believers assembled for public worship; but there is a contrast in the actions of the participants. Suppose that this gathering does not emphasize speaking with tongues but meets as it should for the purpose of prophesying, suggests Paul. He is constantly emphasizing the contrast between unintelligible tongues and prophecy in chapter fourteen.

But if All Prophesy

In stating, "But if all prophesy" Paul is suggesting the all here is the group of individuals present, each one in his proper order. This is indicated as well by the context (vv. 26–33, particularly vv. 27, 30). And the present subjunctive, which was used for the verb "speak" *(lalōsin,* 2980) in verse 23, is also used for the verb "prophesy" *(prophēteúōsin,* 4395), which denotes action in progress, thus also indicating a continuous activity in which one person speaks after another.

Since prophecy is telling forth the counsels of God so that men may understand and obey them, it is in direct contrast to speaking in unknown tongues. Paul seems to be in favor, in certain instances where the whole congregation actively participates, of letting one after another get up and declare God's Word so long as people can understand what they are saying. This is prophesying.

In verse 23 Paul spoke of "those that are unlearned, or unbelievers," using the plural forms. Now, in verse 26, he shifts to the singular: "one that believeth not, or one unlearned." We believe Paul made this change from the plural to the singular deliberately. He is referring to one individual who most likely has never been exposed to a religious meeting of any kind, much less one where people spoke in languages not known to the hearers or in unintelligible ecstatic utterances. The thought is that when many confirmed unbelievers or persons simply ignorant of Christianity come into a gathering of this nature they will be moved to collective ridicule. Derision draws strength from numbers.

Paul seems to ask: "Don't you see to what public condemnation you are exposing the gospel by this practice of speaking non-understandable languages or indulging in ecstatic utterances?" He wants them to recognize the seriousness of the offense. By contrast he points to prophesying, the plain preaching of the gospel, as the means by which conviction comes to the individual heart.

In verse 24, however, which deals with prophesying, Paul reverses the order and speaks first of the "unbeliever" and then of the "unlearned." This indicates that even a heathen, a complete unbeliever, can be convicted by the truth of the gospel when it is preached in a language he can understand.

Also, the word *idiōtēs* (2399, translated "unlearned"), as previously used in this chapter, indicates one who has never been exposed to prophecy, to the preaching of the gospel. Paul knew from his own experience as a preacher that unbelievers are convicted when the gospel is preached plainly and simply.

Paul tells the Corinthians that when they speak in a language that people cannot understand, their hearers will say that they are out of their mind. He speaks as though they were fully aware of this result of their speaking in an unknown tongue. Sadly enough, this did not deter them. "If you loved others," Paul intimates, "you would speak to them clearly, so that they could be won to the Lord Jesus" (a.t.).

He Is Convinced

The conviction of sinners can only be brought about through preaching the gospel to them in words they understand. That is what Paul did; he preached in whatever languages his hearers knew. And the results in the life of an individual hearer were glorious, as Paul declares: "he is convinced of all, he is judged of all: and thus are the secrets of his heart made manifest; and so falling down on his face, he will worship God, and report that God is in (or among) you of a truth" (vv. 24, 25).

According to Paul, conviction has never resulted nor can result from speaking in non-understandable tongues, whether these are naturally or supernaturally learned human languages or ecstatic utterances. Conviction then can result when the believers in the assembly get up and speak forth the truth of Christ in words their hearers can understand. By prophesying he is not referring here to foretelling future events, of course, but to preaching the Word of God, the gospel. One after another, as the prophets of God speak, conviction will come upon the un-believer and upon the uninstructed newborn babe in Christ.

It would appear from verse 24 that this prophesying is not restricted to a chosen few but may be practiced by all believers. The "telling forth" of the grace of God is the mission of every believer and should not be considered the prerogative of the clergy only.

Observe that it is the individual who is being convicted by the testimony of the many. As each one speaks, some new con-viction will come to that individual who is more or less a stranger to the assembly of believers. God often uses the witness of many persons, one complementing the other, to bring full con-viction to an individual heart. Naturally none of us can do all the witnessing or bring about all the convicting needed by those who hear us. God has a place for each of His witnessing children, and we should remember that while He uses our testimony to good effect, He reinforces and supplements it with the witness of others throughout an individual's lifetime. How this should humble us and take away the spirit of jealousy, as we realize both the worth and the incompleteness of our witness in God's scheme of things, as well as the necessity for the witness of others in addition to our own.

The Holy Spirit or Man's Spirit?

Paul speaks of three things that may happen when a person hears the gospel in words that he can understand. First "he is convinced." The word for "convinced" in Greek is *eléngchetai* (1651), the same word the Lord Jesus used in John 16:8, which is translated "reprove," that is, exposed by God for what they re-ally are. "And when he [the Holy Spirit] is come, he will reprove the world of sin, and of righteousness, and of judgment." This is what happened in 1 Corinthians 14:24, where men were at-tracted to and convicted by the Holy Spirit through understandable preaching. What a contrast to the work described in verse 23, the result of man's inflated and misguided spirit.

What does conviction of sin mean? It is the first step of repentance leading to salvation, the realization that one is a sinner in the sight of God. Only the Holy Spirit working upon your spirit through your understanding can bring this about. There can be no conviction without comprehension of your true state. The Greek word for repentance is *metánoia* (3341), "afterthought." The Holy Spirit enables you to look back upon your life and ancestry and see that it is sinful. What Paul brings out here is that the individual sinner cannot exercise afterthought unless he understands what the preacher or prophet is saying. The Holy Spirit and man's own understanding are essential to repentance.

This conviction of the Holy Spirit brings a consciousness of guilt to the souls of believers and unbelievers. This is not the case when the spirit of the individual alone seeks to do the work by speaking a language that others cannot understand. The contrast between the Holy Spirit's work of conviction and man's work of confusion can be seen by considering verse 24 in the light of verse 2. "For he that speaketh in an unknown tongue speaketh not unto men, but unto God: for no man understandeth him; howbeit in the spirit he speaketh mysteries," says Paul in verse 2. And verse 24 presents the contrast he wants them to take to heart and put into practice. "But if all prophesy, and there come in one that believeth not, or one unlearned, he is convinced of all, he is judged of all."

We must not misunderstand the expression in verse 24, "is judged of all"; it does not mean "condemned" or "censured." There are three Greek words that are not always adequately translated in our English versions: *krínein* (2919), which means "to judge"; *katakrínein* (2632), which means "to condemn"; and *anakrínesthai* (350), the verb used here, which is a judicial term meaning cross-examination before a judge in a court of law. Even in Modern Greek, a court hearing is called *anákrisis* (351). "He is cross-examined by all" is the meaning here.

Without understanding there can be no conviction, no consciousness of sin, no edification. Since these are all the fruits of the operation of the Holy Spirit, where these are absent the Holy Spirit is absent. But observe what happens in verse 3: "But he that prophesieth speaketh unto men to edification, and exhortation, and comfort." In verse 3, Paul is speaking of what happens predominantly to believers as a result of prophesying, while in verses 24 and 25 he is referring to the unbeliever; but again he speaks of three things taking place: conviction of sin, judgment, and the revelation of the sinner's innermost secrets.

As the believers in Corinth give one testimony after another bringing out God's requirements for men's lives, this becomes a detailed examination of the life of the unbeliever, to uncover his guilt. The sinner under such conviction often feels that the speaker is aiming directly at him and exposing his sin to others. He often does not realize that it is the Holy Spirit who is leading the preacher to say whatever is needed to bring direct conviction and application to his heart. The speaker can rejoice in this, and should point out to those who take offense at what they believe to be a too particular knowledge of and reference to them that this is only a proof of the Holy Spirit working through the prophet as a channel to reach men's hearts. The probing of God's Word through the prophesying of others should not be taken as applying to someone else but to ourselves, so that we may examine our lives to see if we are obedient to Him.

In John 16:8, where the Lord Jesus speaks of the work of the Holy Spirit, after describing the first result of His operation as reproving the world of sin (conviction), He gives the second result as conviction "of righteousness." The Holy Spirit brings the sinner into the presence of a righteous God before whom he is cross-examined. It is the Holy Spirit's work to take the prophesying of the believers and through it bring about conviction in the heart of a sinner as to the details of his life that are contrary to the righteousness of God. Here again is a vivid contrast between the work of the Holy Spirit through prophesying and the offense brought to others through man's spirit prompting him to speak in non-understandable languages.

Made Manifest

The third effect of prophecy upon the unbeliever through the operation of the Holy Spirit, as given in 1 Corinthians 14:25, is that "the secrets of his heart [are] made manifest." The process of conversion involves self-revelation, self-examination, followed by submission. When we are under conviction, we begin to examine ourselves, and it is then that our secret sins come to the surface and give us no peace until we confess them and lay them at the foot of the cross. These secrets are the motives, the impulses, the tendencies that lie buried under the sinner's words and deeds, such as his lack of love and fear toward God and the absence of love toward his fellowmen, or even his positive enmity against God and hatred and malice toward men. When a sinner is thus convicted and examined he begins to see himself as he is instead of as he would like to appear to himself and others.

What is described here as being effected through prophecy is described in Hebrews 4:12, 13 as being accomplished through the Word of God. "For the word of God is quick, and powerful, and sharper than any two-edged sword, piercing even to the dividing asunder of soul and spirit, and of the joints and marrow, and is a discerner of the thoughts and intents of the heart. Neither is there any creature that is not manifest in his sight: but all things are naked and opened unto the eyes of him with whom we have to do."

Paul's argument is that what the Holy Spirit desires for the unbeliever can be accomplished through the preaching of the Word of God. Why, then, resort to the confusing practice of speaking in non-understandable languages or ecstatic utterances, since these do not convey the Word of God to others? Prophecy must be limited to declaring the Word of God, since it is the Word that produces the desired results of conviction, self-examination, and the bringing to consciousness of one's secret sins. In other words, we need no new revelation, a mysterious revelation through unintelligible speech, but a declaration in plain language of what we already have in the Word of God once and for all delivered to the apostles. It is the Word alone that we must understand and proclaim that others may understand; and when they do, through the activity of the Holy Spirit they will be convicted, they will stand naked before their Judge, they will become conscious of their secret sins.

What will be the result of this in the life of the unbeliever? The inner conviction, the inner cross-examination, the inner revelation of his own sins will find outward expression. "And so falling down on his face, he will worship God, and report that God is in you of a truth" (1 Cor. 14:25). The external act of worship must be preceded by the internal act of the conviction of the Holy Spirit leading to repentance. The words "and so" are *kaí* (2532) *hoútōs* (3778) in Greek, meaning "and as a consequence" or "in the aforementioned manner." As a consequence of this internal act of belief, he will humble himself on his face before God and worship Him. Modern Christianity has lost most of the genuine awe of worship, the sense of the greatness of God and our own insignificance as we approach Him. We do well to realize that when we address God we are not addressing an equal. The utmost reverence should pervade our hearts and be reflected in our posture before Him.

CONVICTION

Do Others See God through Your Witness?

In eastern countries it is customary for people to prostrate themselves, to fall on their faces, when they worship. The Muslims are an example of this. They are not ashamed to assume this humble position even in public. Here, also, the motivation is what counts. Even a position of humility can be assumed for show. Only if it expresses our consciousness of a lack of worth before God, and of obedience and dependence upon Him, is it a worthy act.

In the case of this unbeliever who was convicted as a result of the prophesying in the Corinthian congregation, we see a spontaneous expression of submission and thankfulness to God. Overcome by God's revelation to his own heart, and a sense of his own unworthiness, the sinner falls down before Him in abject surrender. Only the power of the Holy Spirit can produce this complete about-face in the life of a sinner. How different this is from the high-pressure psychology which some modern evangelists use to get people to come forward and make so-called decisions for Christ. No wonder many who make a profession under such human pressures do not remain genuine.

Observe also that the whole focus of worship is God Himself and not the inspired speaker. The gift of prophesying, no matter how successful, is never intended to glorify the possessor of this gift. It is the Spirit of God, not the preacher's own power, that produces results for eternity. Again Paul stresses the contrast between the motive of the one who spoke in non-understandable tongues and the one who prophesied. It is apparent from what Paul said in 1 Corinthians chapter thirteen that the one who spoke in tongues wanted to draw favorable attention to himself, while the one who prophesied recognized that it was only in dependence upon God, through the plain and simple preaching of the gospel, that souls would be saved, and he was willing that God should receive all the glory.

Here, then we have an example of an unbeliever saved as the result of Christian testimony in known understandable languages in the assembly in Corinth. Not only will the convicted sinner fall prostrate on his face and worship God, says Paul, but he will open his mouth to give a public testimony. "He will worship God, and report that God is in you of a truth." This is the confession by mouth that he will make to those who prophesied to him, of which Paul speaks in Romans 10:9, 10. "If thou shalt confess with thy mouth the Lord Jesus, and shalt believe in thine heart that God hath raised him from the dead, thou shalt be saved. For with the heart man believeth unto righteousness; and with the mouth confession is made unto salvation."

Two things stand out here: inner conviction leading to salvation, and outward confession of that which the Holy Spirit has done in the heart. Thus, the unbeliever who came into this service in Corinth goes out a believer. The means of accomplishing this was the gift of prophecy. And the new believer immediately confesses that God is in and among the believers who prophesied to him.

Now what about the seeming discrepancy between verses 22 and 25? In verse 22 Paul says that tongues are for a sign to the unbeliever and that prophesying is for the believer, yet in verse 25 we see that the unbeliever has come to believe, not as a result of tongues but of prophesying. If we consider that verse 22 follows verse 21, which refers to the unbelieving Israelites ("this people"), and realize that this was fulfilled at Pentecost, when the Holy Spirit enabled the disciples to speak in the various languages of Jews from all nations who were present, to proclaim Christ as the Messiah, we shall understand that two different classes of people are involved here. The Jews as a nation rejected

Christ as the Messiah, they rejected this testimony given to them in "other tongues."

But in verses 24 and 25 reference is made to the unbeliever who has not previously heard the gospel and therefore has not had the opportunity to accept or reject it. Furthermore, Paul wanted to point out that if the Jews would not receive the genuine witness of "other tongues" through the supernatural manifestation of the Holy Spirit, the pagans certainly would not receive a spurious manifestation of tongues emanating from man's own spirit. If the genuine manifestation of tongues was ineffectual as far as the unbelieving Jews were concerned, how much less would the spurious manifestation of tongues avail to the conversion of unbelieving pagans. With God's help, the simple act of prophesying, of preaching the gospel in the language of the people, is enough to convert the individual sinner, no matter who he is.

This principle is universally believed in and practiced on the Christian mission field today, even by those groups that believe in speaking in unknown tongues as a result of the infilling of the Holy Spirit. When going to a foreign country, they take time to learn the language of the people to prophesy in and do not depend upon the Holy Spirit to enable them to speak it supernaturally. And it is through prophesying, preaching, witnessing in the language of the hearers, that they expect people to believe.

Of a Truth

What a contrast, Paul declares, between the result of speaking in unknown, non-understandable tongues and the fruits of prophesying in the lives of unbelievers who hear them. Tongues produce the scoffing remark, "You are mad!" Prophecy produces the awed declaration, "Verily, God is in (or among) you!" The word translated "of a truth" in the King James Version is the Greek *óntōs* (3689), meaning "really, actually, in truth." In contrast to his previous unbelief in and denunciation of these people and their God, the new believer now acknowledges that God is in and among them.

Such a confession is evoked in response to prophesying only. It is significantly absent in regard to the person who speaks in non-understandable tongues. Yet the one who speaks in tongues claims to be doing it because of the special manifestation of God's Holy Spirit in and through him. Thus, we conclude that it is not he who says that God is working in and through him who necessarily possesses divine gifts, but the person who, while confessing his own great need of God for his own life, humbly commits himself to serve God with his spirit and with his understanding. It is much better for others to recognize and confess that they see God in our lives than for us to call their attention to our spiritual attainments.

God

In the Greek text, the word for God, *theós* (2316), is preceded by the definite article (*ho* [3588] *theós* [2316], "the God"), which is most significant in the case of this unbeliever. He confesses that he no longer believes in his pagan gods but in the only true God, as a result of the prophesying to which he has listened.

In You

The preposition *en* (1722), in the expression "God is in you," could also be translated "among" you. In this instance, both renderings would be correct and both would apply. In an orderly meeting of Christians where one after the other told forth the Word of God in understandable languages, it would be possible for the hearers to see God among them. As they declared the counsels of God, those whom the Holy Spirit convicted could not but see that what they spoke was the result of what was in their hearts. It was God in them who spoke so convincingly and brought the unbeliever to a saving knowledge of a personal God.

Paul concludes that non-understandable tongues are not only of very little use, they are a hindrance and an offense both to new believers who have not been exposed to them and to unbelievers. If they are to be of any use at all to believers, it is only as they are interpreted, but they are less than useless to the unbeliever. Paul pronounces prophecy far more valuable. It edifies all believers and converts unbelievers. And while speaking in non-understandable tongues can be indulged in to excess, prophesying cannot. Prophesying, unlike unknown tongues, is more likely to be motivated by love to our fellowmen. That is why Paul's great love chapter, 1 Corinthians chapter thirteen, is immediately followed by the words, "Follow after 'love,' and desire spiritual gifts, but rather that ye may prophesy" (14:1). And that is what we, if we are motivated by love for the lost, should covet today: the ability to tell sinners, in plain and understandable words, the way of salvation in Christ.

LESSONS:

1. Paul now presents a different scenario: Suppose at an assembly of the whole congregation at Corinth they were emphasizing prophesying instead of glossolalia.
2. Paul is suggesting that there would be a continuous flow of good teaching, one speaker after another, in an orderly manner (cf. v. 40).
3. Instead of having an embarrassing situation due to uncontrollable, ecstatic utterances, sound declaration of the gospel in understandable terms would convict sincere seekers. A united front should be presented; this would corroborate the gospel message. Glossolalia has the opposite effect.

<table>
<tr><td>

**1 Cor
14:26**

</td><td>

Orderly Participation

</td></tr>
</table>

*How is it then, brethren? when ye come together, every
one of you hath a psalm, hath a doctrine, hath a tongue,
hath a revelation, hath an interpretation. Let all things
be done unto edifying.*

The Proper Use of Spiritual Gifts

In 1 Corinthians 14:1–25, Paul has gone into great detail to
demonstrate the superiority of prophesying over speaking in
unknown tongues or in foreign languages the hearers cannot understand. Undoubtedly, the Christians in Corinth were endowed with various gifts of the Spirit, but in their uninstructed
zeal they needed direction as to how to use them in public worship. As a preliminary to giving them directions for the orderly
exercise of these gifts in the church, he asks the same question
he did in verse 15, "How is it then?" (*Tí* [5101] *oún* [3767]
estín [2076]). "What, then, is" the result of our discussion so far?
Paul was not so much concerned with the fact that the Corinthians had these gifts as with the way they were using them. A spiritual gift is like money in that if you do not use it aright it
would be better if you did not have it at all.

Again Paul demonstrates his love for those whom he seeks
to correct by using the affectionate term "brethren." He indulges

in no derogatory name-calling, as do some who are in disagreement on this issue today. We, too, must be very sure we are in the spirit of 1 Corinthians 13 before we presume to correct the faults of fellow believers as Paul did in chapter fourteen.

When

"When ye come together" indicates the setting of this verse as the local assembly of believers. The adverb *hótan* (3752), "when," could better be translated "whenever," implying that the coming together of the saints of God for worship was a matter of frequent occurrence. While it is true that we can worship God individually at home, this cannot and should not take the place of fellowship with other believers in public worship. Hebrews 10:25 makes it clear that we are not to forsake "the assembling of ourselves together, as the manner of some is."

Every One of You

Paul begins his description of what takes place among the Corinthians in public worship by saying, "Every one hath a psalm." Surely in such a large assembly as that in Corinth, it would be a sheer impossibility for every man, woman, and child to take part. Undoubtedly many came just to hear and not to speak. The natural inference is that "every one" here refers to those who have some spiritual gift and have come prepared to exercise it in public worship. The procedure may have been similar to what takes place in our churches today. "Every one" who is to have a part in the service—members of the choir, the soloist, the speaker or speakers—comes prepared to exercise his or her particular gift. Therefore, the term "every one" should be considered restrictive rather than all-inclusive. It means each one who has a gift and who has come to public worship ready to exercise it.

What were these psalms of which Paul speaks? A psalm, strictly speaking, according to contemporary usage, is a song sung to the harp (Liddell and Scott, p. 2018). They may have been Psalms of David or Christian songs of praise and adoration such as Paul refers to in Ephesians 5:19, where he speaks of "Speaking to yourselves in psalms and hymns and spiritual songs, singing and making melody in your heart to the Lord." We do not know whether this involved singing by a congregation, a choir, or an individual. We do not have any evidence for hymns that were universally accepted by the early Christian church for public worship. But whatever this psalm was, Paul is concerned that it be given forth in a manner to bring edification to the whole group.

Hath

It is interesting to note the repetition of the verb *échei* (2192), "has." Paul's meaning would be better understood if we were to render it, "Every single one of you [who] has a psalm." Not just any one, but every one who had the particular gift could exercise it. This is not a matter of supposition but a statement of fact. Paul indicates that among these Christians are some who have musical ability and have therefore prepared themselves to exercise it in the assembly of believers. Each one is to come to public worship prepared to exercise that gift for which God has best suited him. Preparation is most essential if we are to achieve the utmost in edification of our hearers. This applies to preachers, singers, or any who take part in the worship service of the church. Nor should we seek to usurp the gifts of others, but make the best possible use of the gift(s) God has given us. We are at our best when we are under God, using our very own unique gift from Him and our own method of expression.

There must have been a great variety of spiritual gifts among the Christians in Corinth, making it necessary for the Apostle Paul to lay down rules for using them effectively. What would happen if everyone who had a gift wanted to use it without forethought or planning? Only confusion and disorder could result if each one were to consider himself as under the direct influence of the Holy Spirit and sought to exercise his gift without consideration for others taking part. Many people might attempt to speak at the same time, causing hard feelings and creating an unfavorable impression upon strangers present. Paul seeks to bring order out of this chaos, directing that the participants await their turn, speaking or singing in such a way as to promote harmony rather than disorder. "God is not the author of confusion," he says in concluding his argument on tongues, "but of peace, as in all churches of the saints" (v. 33).

A Psalm

This psalm could not have been sung in a tongue, nor can it be equated with the words of verse 15, "I will sing with the spirit," for it is listed as one of five manifestations in verse 26 that include "a tongue." "Every one of you hath a psalm, hath a doctrine, hath a tongue, hath a revelation, hath an interpretation," says Paul. Since he mentions the psalm first, it is quite possible that this is an indication of how Christians first began their meetings, with singing, thus establishing a good precedent for us to follow in worship services today.

A Doctrine

The next item of Christian worship Paul mentions is teaching, or "doctrine." The Greek word here is *didachḗn* (1322), which can mean both the act and the content of teaching. In the two places where this word occurs in the pastoral epistles (2 Tim. 4:2; Titus 1:9), the passive meaning predominates, which refers to the content of the teaching. There is another Greek word, *didaskalía* (1319), which occurs fifteen times in the pastoral epistles, in which the active meaning is predominant. The Apostle Paul may have used this particular word *didachḗ* (1322) in order to stress his point that it is not only how we say a thing that is important, but also the meaning and content of what we say. The Corinthians seemed to have rather overdone the emotional aspect of worship, and this is what Paul is endeavoring to correct. Great oratorical skill and fervor in witnessing to others cannot take the place of substance.

"Speaking in tongues"—whatever they may be is not the important thing in Christian worship. What is truly important is the edification of others through declaring the whole counsel of God in words that both speaker and hearer can understand.

A Revelation

The third manifestation Paul mentions is "revelation." (In Nestle's Greek text this word precedes the Greek word translated "tongues.") The Greek word *apokalúpsis* (602) does not only refer to something that is entirely new and revelatory of the future but means also "disclosing, manifestation, uncovering, or unveiling of anything hidden." It is taking the lid off something so that we may see and understand it for what it really is. We call the Bible the revelation of God to man, that is, the expression of the mind of God in the language of man for his comprehension. Teaching and revelation actually go hand in hand. Seeing and communicating the meaning in a word, a phrase, an action is a revelation of some truth. We who hold the truth must always endeavor to reveal it to others.

Singing, teaching, revealing—all require the use of speech. In order that they may result in the edification, the upbuilding, of others in the congregation, they must be expressed intelligibly. It would be presumptuous and nonsensical for me to speak in Greek to those who could only comprehend English. Again we come back to the words of Paul, "In the church I had rather speak five words with my understanding, that by my voice I might teach others also, than ten thousand words in an unknown tongue" (v. 19). Let that be our guiding principle also.

Love Seeks to Bring Understanding to Others

As Paul addresses the Corinthian believers in a spirit of love, seeking to set right those things that were causing disturbance in the local church, he mentions five manifestations of worship. We have already considered singing, teaching, and revelation, and now we come to the fourth: speaking in "a tongue."

A Tongue

Does Paul refer to ecstatic utterance here, or to a foreign language? We have observed previously that whenever he uses the plural form, "tongues," he means known human languages, such as he or any other linguist might speak. When he uses the singular form, "tongue," he refers to ecstatic utterances as practiced by the Corinthians.

It is evident from the verses that follow that Paul is not as concerned about the first three manifestations of worship as he is about the speaking in an unknown tongue and the interpretation of such speaking. It is to these last two items that the apostolic command applies: "Let all things be done unto edifying." Singing, teaching, and revelation fulfill this requirement, since they involve the use of man's tongue for communication that will be of benefit to others; but "tongue" here implies unintelligible speech without the exercise of thought or consideration for those who listen.

An Interpretation

Observe that Paul immediately follows "tongue" with "interpretation." As we noted previously, in Nestle's Greek text the order in verse 26 is "psalm, teaching, revelation, tongue, interpretation," and not as the King James Version has translated it, interpolating "revelation" between "tongue" and "interpretation." The word "interpretation" in Greek is *hermēneía* (2058), from which we derive our English word "hermeneutics," meaning the science of interpretation or explanation. The primary meaning of the Greek is to make clear with words something that has been spoken more or less obscurely by others. It is to explain in words, to expound.

The more restricted meaning of *hermēneía* (2058) is a translation into the vernacular of something written or spoken in a foreign tongue. This involves two languages, as when I translate from Greek into English and vice versa. For this I would use the verb *hermēneúō* (2059), meaning "to translate, to interpret," as in John 1:38: "They said unto him, Rabbi, (which is to say, being interpreted or translated [*methermēneuómenon*, 3177 in Nestle's Greek text], Master)." This is translation from Hebrew to Greek, which also occurs in verses 41 and 42, where the words "Messias" and "Cephas" are translated, and in John 9:7, where "Siloam" is interpreted or translated (*hermēneúetai*, 2059).

The substantive *hermēneía* (2058), however, is used only twice in the New Testament, both times in 1 Corinthians in connection with tongues. In 1 Corinthians 12:10 it is used with the plural form ("tongues"). Speaking of the distribution of the gifts of the Spirit, the Apostle in reference to tongues first includes "kinds or families (*génē*, 1085) of languages." This, as we saw in previous studies, refers to a God-given ability to learn foreign families of languages, such as the Semitic, the Germanic, the African, and so forth. The other gift is the aforementioned *hermēneía* (2058) *glōssōn* (1100), "interpretation of languages." Does this mean the interpretation of the Corinthian "unknown tongues" into a human, understandable language, or does it rather refer to the ability to translate one human, intelligible language into another so that it may become meaningful to those who hear it? This latter is a real gift, for though you may know two languages well, you may not be able to render one into another fluently. I have often seen the truth of this in Greece, when a visiting English-speaking preacher came to address the Greek brethren. In one congregation there may be several who know Greek and English equally well, yet only one or two will have the gift of good and acceptable interpretation from English into Greek. And quite often they cannot do the reverse, translate acceptably from Greek into English. There is no doubt that the faithful translation of thoughts through words from one language into another is a real gift of God.

It was for the ability to speak in known languages that Paul praised God, in verse 18. But he never seemed to find it necessary to translate for anyone who preached, nor do we find any record of his ever acting as an interpreter. It may be that wherever this great apostle went, he did the preaching, and since he was a truly gifted linguist he could speak whatever language was understood by the majority of his hearers. Although he was a Hebrew, he must have done most of his preaching in Greek. But though Paul never had to make use of the gift of interpretation, others would certainly need it in the years ahead. Both the speaking and translating of foreign languages are real gifts of God and have been of inestimable value to missionaries down through the centuries in the proclamation of the gospel.

But when we come to 1 Corinthians 14:26, it is a different matter. "Any one of you . . . has a tongue" refers to the unknown ecstatic utterances of the Corinthians that Paul condemns. He does so primarily on the ground that they do others no good, their sole benefit being an emotional one to the speaker himself. He says most emphatically that no one is to speak in an unknown tongue unless there is an interpreter present. He thus implies that when the hearer cannot understand then he can derive no possible benefit. Therefore, to provide at least a possibility of edification, interpretation is necessary.

This is the only condition under which speaking in tongues could be tolerated, and it would be acceptable then only to the fellow believers of the Corinthians and not to unbelievers. The unbelievers would reason that a person who could speak understandably and yet chose to use an unknown tongue was not in his right mind. But the mature believer who heard an interpretation of such ecstatic utterances might conceivably find some edification in it. The unbeliever needs life before maturity. That is why Paul tells the Corinthians, in a spirit of loving tolerance, that if they insist on this matter of ecstatic utterances they must limit their practice to the circle of believers, and then only if an interpreter is present. He does not recommend it, but he tolerates it as the lesser of two evils, the greater evil being speaking in an unknown tongue before mixed groups of believers and unbelievers, and without an interpreter.

Since Paul's burden right along has been the practice of speaking in an unknown tongue, there must have been some who indulged in this practice without anyone making their utterances meaningful to others by interpreting them. "If any of you have a tongue" indicates that such people came to worship apparently ready to speak in this kind of ecstatic utterance. What eagerness there must have been to show off this so-called gift among the Corinthians.

And apparently there were those among them who had what they thought was the gift of being able to understand this unknown tongue and interpret it. Now it follows that, if the speaking in tongues proceeded from man's own spirit, the interpretation is equally a human fabrication.

Paul takes this state of affairs as it were. He presents to the Corinthians the more excellent way of love, which demands utmost consideration of others. At least, he implies, if you feel you are saying something when you speak with tongues, let someone interpret, so that others may benefit if possible. The content of thought is more important than the manner of expressing it. Paul was not so much concerned with eradicating this practice as he was with instilling love for others as a guiding principle that would ultimately lead these Corinthians to abolish on their own any practices that involved disregard for others. Paul knew that an order from someone else to correct ourselves is never as effective as personal conviction about the error of our ways.

LESSONS:

1. In a large meeting it is impossible for every person to participate. Paul instructs the gifted individuals to lead the public worship, as long as general mutual edification results.
2. This assumes that some preparation and forethought should precede the exercise of each gift. Otherwise, confusion and disorder may occur.
3. Paul is advocating that intelligible speech be expressed in singing, in teaching, and in revealing.

1 Cor. 14:27, 28

Control It!

> *If any man speak in an unknown tongue, let it be by two, or at the most by three, and that by course; and let one interpret. But if there be no interpreter, let him keep silence in the church; and let him speak to himself; and to God.*

Regulate Your Tongue

Paul singles out speaking in an unknown tongue as the offending element in the worship services at Corinth. In 1 Corinthians 14:26 he how these services taking place, not how they ideally should be. Now, in verses 27 and 28, he sets forth certain regulations that should govern this practice if it does take place. "And (consequently) if" (*eite*, 1535) is how verse 27 begins in the Greek, indicating a concession on the part of Paul. "And if any man speak in an unknown tongue," here is how it should be done. "Let it be by two, or at the most by three, and that by course; and let one interpret." Since the word "tongue" here is singular in number, we conclude that it refers to ecstatic utterances, as has been the trend throughout Paul's discussion.

By Two, or at the Most by Three

Paul's first stipulation is that if this ecstatic speaking takes place it should be "by two, or at the most by three." He is concerned lest so many would want to get up to speak in tongues that there would be no time left for the other manifestations of worship. Anyone may speak with tongues, he declares, but do not let too many participate. The King James Version says "by two, or at the most by three." The word "by" does not adequately render the meaning of the Greek preposition *katá* (2596) here, which is distributive. *Katá* refers also to the "meeting" and not only to the people who speak in an unknown tongue. *Katá* in this context refers to the number of people who may speak at a meeting. The whole context seems to imply that no more than two or three may speak in tongues at any one meeting, and no more than one may speak at a time. The thought is, "In each meeting let there be two, or at the most three, who speak." It places a limitation on the number of people who can engage in this practice at any one worship service.

It would be difficult to understand the meaning here if the preposition *katá* (2596) referred to the number "two or three." It could not mean that two or at the most three people would be permitted to stand up and speak simultaneously, for this would defeat the purpose of the regulation (which was to eliminate confusion), unless, of course, all the speakers said the same thing. There is no evidence that speaking in an unknown tongue was ever practiced in this orderly fashion, as we engage in Scripture reading or hymn singing in unison today. If it were, why condemn the Corinthians?

By Course

The second regulation is "and that by course." In Greek this is *kaí* (2532) *aná* (303) *méros* (3313), "and in turn." This second rule precludes the possibility of the first rule meaning that two or three may speak simultaneously. Apparently the Corinthian Christians were so eager to show off this new accomplishment that they interrupted one another, a breach of good manners that we do not allow our children to commit, much less do we condone in public worship.

And Let One Interpret

The third rule is "And let one interpret." This would not necessarily be the same person interpreting for each one who spoke in a tongue. The word *heís* (1520), "one," is used here for the same reason as rule two, to limit the number who should take part. No two interpreters should speak simultaneously. As soon as one person finishes speaking in a tongue not understood by the congregation, let someone interpret it. It may be that there were as many in Corinth ready to demonstrate what they thought was their gift of interpretation as there were those who were eager to show off what they thought to be the gift of tongues. There is no indication that there was just one interpreter at a meeting, and actually there is nothing in Paul's discussion to exclude one and the same person from speaking in a tongue and also interpreting what he had said, as suggested in verse 13: "Let him that speaketh in an unknown tongue pray that he may interpret."

The meaning becomes clearer if we take the word *heís* (1520, one) to mean "a single one" or "one alone." "Let anyone interpret," says Paul (with the unspoken implication, "if he can"). He knew that this Corinthian tongue-speaking was devoid of thought and therefore could not be made meaningful by interpretation. Such interpretation could only be guesswork and therefore valueless.

Paul's third stipulation brings him one step closer to making these Corinthians realize the futility of this whole business of tongues and their interpretation. "But if there be no interpreter," he says in verse 28, "let him keep silence in the church; and let him speak to himself, and to God." Paul's argument continually revolves around the thesis that only what is understood can edify. But how could the speaker in an unknown tongue know in advance whether there would be anyone in the congregation able to interpret what he might say and thus make it understandable to others? If tongue-speaking were reducible to uniform phonetic sounds, he could be sure of this; but since it is not, he would have no way of knowing. Paul knew that when the Corinthians spoke in a tongue, very often no one present was able to interpret. This, therefore, may only be a polite way of saying, "Since you cannot be sure in advance that what you will utter in an unknown tongue can be interpreted by someone, do not engage in this practice in public at all." Do not be caught in the predicament of having said something in the presence of the assembled worshipers which no one can understand or make understandable. Do not take even a remote chance of bringing scandal upon the congregation.

This speaking in a tongue and interpreting it is not the same thing at all as the gifts of the Spirit that Paul mentions in 1 Corinthians 12:10. The "diverse kinds of tongues" and "the interpretation of tongues" that he speaks of there refer to the God-given ability to speak or to interpret various families of languages other than one's own, such as the Semitic, Germanic, Latin, and so forth. The contrast between this and what Paul is speaking about in 1 Corinthians 14:28 is that the former deals with known, human languages, whose interpretation is a matter of the rules of translation: while the latter refers to non-human, non-intelligible utterances, never consistently the same, whose interpretation is a matter of guesswork.

If There Be No Interpreter

Therefore, the hypothetical conjunction, *eán* (1437) *mē* (3361), "if not," with which verse 28 begins, takes on the meaning of "unless." "But unless there can be no interpreter, let him who speaks in an unknown tounge keep silence in the church" (a.t.). It took Paul a long time to say it, but in verse 28 he makes it final and imperative. This is what he has been driving at right along, trying to make the Corinthians realize that unless they can make themselves readily understood in the assembly, it is better to keep quiet.

If God could enable someone to speak in an unknown tongue, but permitted him to do so only when an interpreter was present who could make what he said understandable to others, why should He not have made it understandable in the first place? We have no record of God ever having spoken in a language intelligible to no one. Why should He enable His children to do so, since whether He speaks to men directly or indirectly He wants them to understand what He says? Once again we are driven back upon the conclusion that both the speaking with a tongue and the interpretation of it were manifestations of man's emotional nature and emanated solely from his own spirit.

What, then, is a believer to do who feels this desire to speak in an unknown tongue? "Let him speak to himself," says Paul (not silently in his own heart, but in privacy giving vent to sounds of ecstasy), "and to God" (that is, in prayer). Audible prayer can be very helpful, not only when ecstatic sounds are involved but when we commune with God in the ordinary way. But to God it is not the words that matter but our attitude of heart before Him. Whether we speak in humanly understandable sounds or not, He can discern our state.

Prayer is primarily between man and God and not something we engage in for the admiration of others. When we pray in public, others are supposed to join in mentally. This is communion, not consciously between human beings but between humans and the divine. Paul expressed the same thought in verse 4: "He that speaketh in an unknown tongue edifieth himself; but he that prophesieth edifieth the church." An ecstatic experience in prayer may be uplifting to the one who has it but to no one else. Therefore, let it be confined to private worship. In such a circumstance you need no interpretation of what you say, whatever the language could be.

LESSONS:

1. Here the Apostle Paul was singling out "speaking in an unknown tongue." He was attempting to bring it under control by placing a limitation on the number and the order of those who were allowed to engage in this practice at any one worship service.
2. Paul would not allow simultaneous tongue-speaking because this type of one-upmanship was very ill-mannered.
3. Paul knew that the Corinthians' glossolalia could not be interpreted. Any attempt to do so would be valueless. He hoped that this exercise in futility would teach them a valuable lesson. If God could speak in an "unknown" tongue, but only when an "interpreter" were present, why would He not make the message understandable in the first place, thus avoiding one complete step?
4. Paul's main point is: Only what is understood can edify.

| 1 Cor. 14:29–31 | *An Atmosphere of Order* |

Let the prophets speak two or three, and let the other judge. If anything be revealed to another that sitteth by, let the first hold his peace. For ye may all prophesy one by one, that all may learn, and all may be comforted.

The Preacher Must Be Considerate

After Paul had set forth the regulations for speaking in an unknown tongue, concluding with the admonition that this practice should not be undertaken in public, he goes on to contrast it with prophesying. This is still in the context of public worship, "when you come together" (v. 26).

You remember how strange it seemed that Paul omitted the word "prophecy" when he listed the manifestations of public worship (v. 26). He mentioned "a psalm, a doctrine, a revelation, a tongue, an interpretation," and went right on to talk about the last two items. Now (v. 29), he resumes the subject of prophecy, as he gives directions for the prophets. Of what did their prophesying consist? Quite probably the other three items, all of which have to do with the spoken word. Psalm, doctrine, and revelation would correspond to singing, teaching, and exhortation—all included in the comprehensive term, "prophecy."

Let the Prophets Speak

Actually, in the Greek, verse 29 begins with an adversative. "But the prophets two or three let them speak." What is the contrast here, since apparently the same thing was said about speaking in a tongue? For one thing, the absolute limit on the maximum number is missing. Paul suggests that two or three prophets speaking at any one meeting would be adequate. Even with regard to prophecy, he feels that there can be too much of a good thing. Consideration for others should lead the prophets not to prolong the service unduly. This is good advice for us preachers, who sometimes are so concerned with giving out all we know that we get carried away by our own emotions and enthusiasm.

Another lesson that we might learn from this verse is the desirability of having more than one person participate in audible public worship. A preacher should encourage the congregation as individuals to take part in offering a prayer, a psalm, exhortation, and not do everything himself, but hold the number down to two or three.

The real contrast of verses 27–29, however, lies in the fact that where prophesying is concerned there is no "if" involved. With regard to speaking in an unknown tongue, there was a restriction: "If there be no interpreter . . . keep silence in the church." But since a prophet always speaks in a known language, there is no time when he need be silenced in public worship.

And Let the Other Judge

The second part of verse 29, "and let the other judge," is made clearer by an examination of the Greek text. First, the word "the other" is actually plural, *hoi* (3588) *álloi* (243) that is, "the others." This refers to the balance of the prophets, those who have not had an opportunity to speak; they are supposed to do the judging.

The word "judge" also needs clarifying, lest it be construed as censorious criticism. In Greek it is *diakrinētōsan* (1252), which should be translated "discern" or "interpret." To discern actually means "to have the ability to see what is not evident to the average mind." This is a gift of God ("discerning of spirits," as mentioned in 1 Cor. 12:10), the ability to detect, distinguish, or discriminate what lies back of a man's words or works, "in order to determine whether they truly proceed from the Holy Spirit or whether they represent pretenses of the human spirit or contain the deception of some spirit of evil. All Christians are to 'prove the spirits, whether they are of God'; but certain difficult cases occur, for which more than common Christian discernment is necessary. False prophets love to use deceptive language. For the purpose of unmasking these prophets the Lord provides this gift and thus enables His church to turn from lying spirits to the one Spirit of truth" (Lenski, R. H., *The Interpretation of 1 and 2 Corinthians*. Minneapolis, MN: Augsburg Publishing House, 1971:503,504).

Many believers, and even preachers, who know the Lord and believe the Bible to be the Word of God, unfortunately lack the ability to discern whether others are true or false prophets. In the pews of a great number of theologically-unsound churches sit many saints of God who listen uncritically week after week, while the preacher gives forth less than the whole counsel of God, and feel that nothing is wrong. These brethren lack the gift of discernment. How we need to pray for this gift today, when there is such widespread departure from the truth of God's Word and where dishonest handling of Biblical terms is deceiving even some of God's elect.

Hold His Peace

Verse 31 implies that the prophets also need to be curbed from showing off, "If anything be revealed to another that sitteth

by, let the first hold his peace." Paul advises the speaker who is
tempted to monopolize the spotlight not to think that he is the
only one who has a revelation from God, but to speak briefly and
be willing to give someone else a chance.

The verb *apokaluphthē* (601), "be revealed," is in the passive
voice, indicating a definite revelation to the one who wants to
speak, not from himself but from the Holy Spirit. It would be
wrong to interrupt a speaker just for the sake of introducing our
pet ideas and theories in public worship. Also note that this revelation is not given to be communicated in an unknown tongue
but is connected with the gift of prophesying, which is always
in a known language. Otherwise, the gift of discernment could
not be exercised.

In verse 31, Paul goes on to express a permission regarding
prophecy that he never granted with respect to tongues. "For ye
may all prophesy one by one, that all may learn, and all may be
comforted." The emphasis here is not on "all" but on "ye may."
If we connect this with the previous verse, we see that what Paul
says is, "If any one prophet does not take too much time, then
you will all have a chance to prophesy." Of course, the principle
is that each one may prophesy in turn, two or three at a meeting, until each has had an opportunity.

That All May Learn

But, says Paul, keep in mind the purpose of such prophesying.
This purpose, expressed by the Greek telic word *hína* (2443, so
that or in order that) is twofold: that each one in the local congregation who listens to you may learn, and that each may be
comforted. No one can learn anything from listening to an unknown tongue. The Greek word for "learn" is *manthánōsin* (3129),
which of course is akin to *mathētēs* (3101), meaning "disciple" or
"student." When we prophesy or preach, we must teach, so that
others may learn something that will further glorify God and be

life-transforming, which they did not know before. It is the preacher's duty to take time to unearth fresh facts and inspiration from the Word of God for the hearts and minds of his people. Learning is the first purpose of prophesying, for it is by learning that we come to believe and are edified. The gospel of the Lord Jesus Christ presents a challenge that can stand up to any human intelligence. To the honest intellect it can reveal its own inadequacy when measured against the supreme Intelligence.

And All May Be Comforted

The second purpose of prophesying is "that all may be comforted." The Greek verb *parakaleō* (3870) may mean not only "to comfort" but "to appeal, to urge, to exhort, to admonish." God's Word is not only full of comfort for the believer, which the preacher is to minister to his flock, but it also contains much in the way of exhortation and admonition. This second meaning fits in better with the purpose of learning. The prophet is not only to teach but to urge his hearers to appropriate and apply what has been learned. Prophesying must apply to the reason and the will.

It is interesting that all three verbs in this verse prophesy, learn, and comfort or admonish—are not in the aorist tense in Greek, which would indicate a once-and-for-all matter. In other words, not all who prophesy can expect to do so at one meeting, but at some meeting they will get their turn. Not all that should be known can be learned at any one meeting. Not all the comfort and admonition God has for us can be appropriated at any one meeting. We have here a continuous process of prophesying, of learning, of comfort and admonition. At every occasion of public worship there must be opportunity for these; and the more we experience the more we feel we need. We can never be fully taught, fully comforted, fully admonished. It is an ignorant person who thinks he knows it all. Let us remember this, whether we mount the pulpit or take our place in the pews.

LESSONS:

1. Note that Paul allows a Christian prophet to be interrupted.
2. Since an inspired teacher (a prophet) always spoke in a known language, there was no need for him to be silenced in public worship.
3. The other prophets who were listening carefully had the gift of discernment (1 Cor. 12:10) in order to detect error or evil motives.
4. If the designated prophets do not take all the time, then all the other prophets might have a chance to prophesy.

1 Cor. 14:32, 33 | *Peace*

And the spirits of the prophets are subject to the prophets.
For God is not the author of confusion, but of peace, as in
all churches of the saints.

Self-control and God's Control

When Paul says that the spirits of the prophets are under their own control, he is contrasting this with his previous observation that those who spoke in unknown tongues gave the impression of being "mad," which in the Greek means under the control of an influence outside oneself (see v. 23). That the prophet of God is in control of his reasoning faculties is also indicated in verse 30, where Paul says that, when more than one person desires to speak, after a reasonable time each speaker should hold his peace to give the next person a chance. You need to exercise your mental faculties to know when to hold your peace, that is, to stop talking.

Subject to the Prophets

Now in verse 32 Paul comes out with the unequivocal statement that a prophet is in full control of his mental faculties. When a prophet speaks with the purpose of teaching, comforting, and admonishing others, he is exercising his mind. He has purpose in his prophesying, which cannot be said of one who speaks in a tongue that others cannot understand. Since the prophet is speaking forth God's revelation, it is evident that, when our spirits are controlled and directed by God's Spirit, they do not lose the function of thinking and deciding. Man possessed by God does not lose his identity. Self-control is part of God's control of us. When we lack self-control, we cannot claim to be God-controlled.

When Paul says that the spirits of the prophets are subject to the prophets, he does not mean that the spirits of the speaking prophets are subject to the prophets who hear them, but that the spirits of the ones speaking are subject to their own control. The word "spirits" here refers to that part of man that thinks and wills. When that comes under the control of someone else, he is no longer self-controlled. He ceases to be responsible for what he does and cannot give direction and purpose to what he says, so that his speech will serve to teach and admonish others.

Paul's thesis throughout has been that when the believer speaks in the assembly of other believers, they must understand him. This requires, among other things, that when one person is speaking, others must keep quiet. More than one may speak during the service, but each in turn. Paul has consistently condemned speaking in an unknown tongue, especially when there is no interpreter because the basic purpose of speech would be defeated. Speaking in an unknown tongue produces just as much confusion as several people speaking in known languages all at once.

Having urged the prophets to exercise self-control, Paul goes on to give the motivation and reason for this in verse 33: "For God is not the author of confusion, but of peace." Here is what God is, he tells them. You are supposed to be like Him. God gave you your mind and will in order to produce orderliness. Do not stop using them. In other words, God expects you to exercise self-control. Whenever confusion and disorderliness are the product of your speaking, you can rest assured that you are not in control of your own spirit, nor is God in control of it. God would not inspire you to say one thing and another person another, at one and the same time.

The Author of Confusion

The word "confusion" is a very strong one in Greek, *akatastasías* (181), meaning "instability, a state of disturbance, anarchy." In James 3:15, we learn that this is the result of the wisdom that is "earthly, sensual, devilish." James says, "For where envying and strife is, there is confusion and every evil work" (James 3:16). Actually, the words translated "envying" and "strife" in Greek are *zélos* (2205) and *eritheía* (2052), which could be more adequately translated "zeal," or "jealousy," or "eagerness," and "party-strife." Those who are possessed of this false, earthly wisdom, James says, are also possessed with the zeal to propagate it. The zeal to propagate a falsehood sometimes far exceeds the zeal to propagate truth.

This is what really lay heavy on Paul's heart as he winds up his argument about the practice of speaking in tongues. There is no doubt that the Corinthians were zealous. The confusion they caused was due to their great enthusiasm over a phenomenon they misunderstood to be a manifestation of the Holy Spirit. Paul opens their eyes to the harm they are doing and strongly urges them to seek the edification of the whole congregation rather than their own self-gratification as individuals. By continuing to speak unintelligibly in the assembly, Paul warns them, you are bringing God into disrepute. Your own reputation alone was at stake, it would not be so bad. However, these Corinthians were attributing their ecstatic experiences to God, the Holy Spirit. This is what causes grief to the Apostle.

This confusion, he tells them, is the product of your misguided zeal and desire for admiration.

That brings us to the second word James uses as the cause of confusion, *eritheía* (2052), translated "strife." This noun comes from the verb *eritheúomai*, which was used of those who intrigued or canvassed for office, courting popular applause by trickery and low arts. "Party-spirit" would probably best convey its meaning. And as we read Paul's letter to the Corinthians, we can readily see that these were people not only of misguided zeal but of partisanship. The confusion among them was augmented by the desire to show off.

This ability to speak in an unknown tongue must have seemed quite a spectacular accomplishment. What a subtle temptation for those who engaged in it to do so with one eye to the gallery. An even more grievous thing than sin itself is to do an ostensibly good act from sinful and sensual motives, attributing it to God. Ask yourself why you really do and say what you do, what your underlying motives are for all your words. Acting from selfish motives may bring exaltation to yourself, but it can only lead to confusion for others, who will think less of God as a result.

That thought should really horrify us—that as a result of our zealous, self-centered behavior others should come to think less of God. Let us purify our motives, and conduct ourselves in such a manner that those around us, believers and unbelievers alike, will think of God as the author of peace.

Paul loved to ascribe the appellation "God of peace" to his heavenly Father, and desired his life and worship to show Him forth to others as "the God of all peace." Before speaking in tongues or saying or doing anything before others, let us ask ourselves, "Will this reflect on God as the author of confusion or of peace?" Then and then only should we proceed.

LESSONS:

1. Unlike the speakers of an "unknown" tongue who were out of control, the Christian prophets were to be in full control of their faculties.
2. The prophets in Corinth were capable of stopping their speeches.
3. According to 2 Peter 1:20, 21, ". . . the prophecy came not in old time by the will of man: but holy men of God spake as they were moved by the Holy Ghost." In other words, when God revealed Himself to these men, they did not lose their identities, vocabularies, or sense of judgment, yet they were totally submissive to God's control of them.
4. God expected the Christian prophets to exercise the same kind of self-control to produce orderliness, without surrendering their minds and wills. Misguided enthusiasm must not be allowed to reign.

PEACE

| 1 Cor. 14:33 | *Order Should Characterize God's People* |

For God is not the author of confusion but of peace, as in all churches of the saints.

Having urged the prophets to exercise self-control, Paul goes on to give the motivation and reason for this by describing the character of God.

"For God Is Not the Author of Confusion"

"For" as is the translation of the Greek particle *gár* (1063) provides the reason that the practice of speaking in an unknown tongue cannot be attributed to God or His Spirit as its author or initiator. The Corinthians who spoke in an unknown tongue were claiming that their speech was motivated by God's Spirit. God's Spirit is God Himself. The argument which Paul provides is that the situation in the Corinthian worship was disturbing. There was a lack of peace, and therefore it could not be of God because God is not a God of confusion nor does He produce confusion. One need only look at nature to confirm this. There is an order in it. Different varieties of trees have different leaves and a different bark and yield different fruit, yet they are all trees. The same order is true in the animal, fowl and fish kingdoms. While there is a wide variety within each group, each still has its distinct pattern and form. A whole book could be written proving this point alone, but the open-minded and intelligent person can easily come to this conclusion without persuasive arguments. The God of creation is a God of intelligent order.

This verse actually begins in Greek with the negative *ou* (3756), not. Paul dogmatically states that it is absolutely inconceivable for the God of the Bible, the creator of the world, to be a God of haphazard character and action. The challenge of the great Apostle is for us, the cognitive creatures of God, to consider this world He has made. It is orderly. We can base ourselves on its past performance and draw our expectations for the future. We know, for instance, what time the sun is going to rise tomorrow morning and what time it is going to set. We can know what time the tide will come in and what time it will go out. God is not, absolutely not, a God of instability (*akatastasía* [181]). He is not like the Pythia, the priestess of the mythological worship Apollo at Delphi, who delivered ambiguous oracles. God is a God of logic and order and means what He says and says what He means.

In Corinth, when the unknown tongue was spoken, it had no logical meaning. It could not be tested linguistically. If it had a set meaning, it would be possible for it to be heard by two different interpreters who both would give the same translation independently of one another. If the interpretation of one saying can mean more than one thing, then confusion results. That is what was happening in Corinth where the practice of speaking in an unknown tongue took place. When Pythia spoke, it could be interpreted by different people to mean different things. It did not have a concrete meaning and left its hearers in a state of bewilderment. But that is not the character of the God of the Bible. When He speaks, it is for the purpose of being understood, to guide us into actions that are for our good and His glory. Thus Paul plainly declares that God is not the author of confusion. He speaks the truth, and Christ who became the true Revealer of God affirmed that He is the truth (John 14:6; 1 John 5:20).

In the statement "For God is not" the Greek text has "the God" (*ho* [3588], the, the definite article denoting the uniqueness of the God of the Bible as revealed by the Lord Jesus Christ; *Theós* [2316], God). The Greek verb is *estín,* the third person singular present indicative of *eimí* (1510), to be. This use of present tense is called the gnomic present, which means that it is true at all times. It pertains to the unchangeable character of God and not how He acted in a particular circumstance and time. As Paul says in 2 Corinthians 1:20, "For all the promises of God in Him are yes, and in Him Amen, unto the glory of God by us." This means that if God's children bear God's character, they reveal who God really is by what they say. That is what the word "glory" (*dóxa* [1391]) means. It comes from the verb *dokéō* (1380), to think, to recognize. If we are orderly people, others will recognize that the God, whose we are and whom we worship, is the God of order.

"The author" is in italics in the King James Version because it is not in the Greek text. It is an interpretive insertion. The word "confusion" is very strong in Greek. It is *akatastasías,* the genitive of *akatastasía* meaning instability or a state of disturbance and tumult. It derives from the privative *alpha* (1), without, and the noun *katástasis* (n.f.), which means a settling, a settled condition. The compound word, therefore, means a disturbed state, a state without order. In Luke 21:9 it is translated "commotions"; in 1 Corinthians 14:33 and James 3:16, "confusion," and in 2 Corinthians 6:5; 12:20, "tumults."

In James 3:15, we learn that this confusion is the result of the wisdom that is "earthly, sensual, devilish." James says, "For where envying and strife is, there is confusion [*akatastasía*] and every evil work" (James 3:16). The instability caused by haughty attitudes toward others emanates from a self-supposed preeminence over our fellowmen. Actually, the word translated "envying" in Greek is *zélos* (2205) which could be translated more adequately as "zeal" or "jealousy." The word "strife" is *eritheía* (2052), party spirit or contention. Those who are possessed of this false, earthly wisdom, James says, are also possessed with the zeal to propagate it. The zeal to propagate falsehood sometimes far exceeds the zeal to propagate truth, for Satan provides his followers with relentless fury. This noun comes from the verb *eritheúomai* (n.f.) which was used of those who entreated or canvassed for office, courting popular applause by trickery and questionable methods. "Party spirit" would probably best convey its meaning. And as we read Paul's letter to the Corinthians, we can readily see that these were people not only possessed of misguided zeal, but of partisanship (1 Cor. 1:11–13). The confusion among them was augmented by the desire to show off.

The ability to speak in an unknown tongue must have seemed quite a spectacular accomplishment. What a temptation for those who engaged in it to do so with pride. An even more grievous thing than a sin itself is to do a good act from sinful and sensual motives, attributing them to God. Ask yourself why you really do and say what you do and say, what your underlying motives are for all your words and actions. Acting from selfish motives may bring exaltation to yourself, but it can only lead to confusion for others who will think less of God as a result.

This disturbance and tumult lay heavily on Paul's heart as he ended his written discourse regarding the practice of speaking in an unknown tongue or in foreign languages without interpretation. There is no doubt that the Corinthians were zealous. The confusion they caused was due to their great enthusiasm over a phenomenon they misunderstood to be a manifestation of the Holy Spirit. Paul opens their eyes to the harm they are doing and strongly urges them to seek the edification of the whole congregation rather than their own self-gratification as individuals (1 Cor. 14:3, 5, 12, 26). By continuing to speak unintelligibly in the assembly, Paul warns them, they are bringing God into disrepute. If it were only their own reputation that was at stake, it would not be so bad. However, these Corinthians were mistakenly attributing their ecstatic experience to the Holy Spirit. This brought grief to the Apostle.

In our verse, confusion is presented as the opposite of peace (*eirēnē* [1515]). This means that God is the author of peace, not that He needs peace for Himself, but that He is the dispenser of peace (John 14:27; 16:33; Rom. 1:7; 14:17; 15:33; 1 Cor. 7:15; Eph. 4:3; Heb. 12:14).

In 2 Corinthians 6:5 in describing the afflictions of the minister of the gospel, *akatastasíai* has the meaning of unsettled conditions and uncertainties as to the place where he makes his residence. A minister of the gospel may find it necessary to move around in his endeavor to evangelize people.

In 2 Corinthians 12:20 *akatastasíai* (pl.) is translated "tumults" (KJV) and describes the unsettled attitudes of the Corinthians because of debates, envyings, wraths, strifes, backbitings, whisperings and spiritual swellings or pride. Paul here describes the quarrelsome lifestyle which characterized the Corinthian believers.

In Luke 21:9 the word *akatastasíai* is translated "commotions" because these were the result of a state of war and refers to the external circumstances created by troubled times.

"But of Peace"

Christian worship was established by God, and, since He is a God of order, He wants to be worshiped in an orderly manner.

Paul loved to ascribe the appellation "God of peace" to his heavenly Father and desired his life and worship to show Him forth to others as the "God of all peace." In this Corinthian passage (14:33) "peace" (*eirēnēs*) means a state of tranquility

(Luke 2:29; 11:21; John 16:33; Acts 9:31; 1 Thess. 5:3). It is the opposite of commotion or confusion (*akatastasía*). The word *eirḗnē* can have the noun *katástasis* as a synonym which, however, does not occur in the New Testament. The word means a settling down, a quieting or calming. God is a God of a settled spirit, a calming effect upon those who experience His grace. In fact, Scripture tells us that the gift of His grace is peace (1 Cor. 1:3; 2 Cor. 1:2; Gal. 1:3; Eph. 1:2; Phil. 1:2; Col. 1:2; 1 Thess. 1:1; 2 Thess. 1:2; 1 Tim. 1:2; 2 Tim. 1:2; Titus 1:4; Phil. 3).

"As"

The Greek word translated "as" is *hōs* (5613), a relative adverb meaning "in the same manner as." Here Paul stresses the difference that existed and could be observed easily in the public worship of Corinth as contrasted with all the other existing churches Paul knew. The only church that was different was the church in Corinth. In all the other churches, the worshiper left with the impression that the God worshiped was a God of peace, not of instability, one saying one thing and another something different as in the church of Corinth, yet claiming that it all came from God.

How peaceful is the God you worship? Do you give others the impression that He is the one who causes you to be out of control and speak at the top of your voice? The Psalmist says, "The Lord will give strength unto His people; the Lord will bless His people with peace" (Ps. 29:11). We do not only have peace as a result of God's presence in us, but we are to "seek peace, and pursue it" (Ps. 34:14). Do you seek a church where God is worshiped in peace or in confusion and noise as in Corinth?

"In All the Churches"

Christ established one Church, the redeemed people from all walks of life, races, colors, irrespective of gender (Gal. 3:28). It is His Church (Matt. 16:18) over which He exercises His love and care. The saved people who meet in any one place for the worship of God in Christ constitute a local church, and they bear a tremendous responsibility in the way they worship God.

"Churches" here in Greek has the definite article "the" in front of the word. They are the churches, the body of Christ, assembled believers meeting in one locality such as in Ephesus, Philippi, Thessalonica, and so on. "In all" is *pásais,* the dative plural feminine adjective of *pás* (3956), all, and it means in all the local churches Paul knew.

It is to be observed that each body of believers constitutes "the Church" of Jesus Christ. When Paul introduces himself to the church in Corinth, he calls it "the church of God which is at Corinth" (1 Cor. 1:2). A feeling of awe should consume us in knowing that the God we worship is the God of the total Christian Church.

"Of the Saints"

Paul is careful in describing all the other churches as "churches of the saints" (*tṓn,* the genitive plural masculine article *ho,* the; *hagíōn,* the genitive plural masculine adjective of *hágios* [40], saint). Paul calls the people who are gathered together to worship God in one place not only a local church (*ekklēsía* [1577]), but the gathering together of the "saints." A saint is one who is distinguished by a character that is separate or holy, and has the holiness (*hagiótes* [41], inherent holiness of God) of God through sanctification (*hagiasmós* [38]) unto God. This automatically invokes separation from evil. Paul involves moral integrity.

LESSONS:

1. We bear a personal responsibility in selecting the group with whom we worship.

2. Our worship services should demonstrate that the God we believe in and worship is the God of peace and not of instability.
3. The church of Corinth constituted an exception to peace. It was noisy and factious and was confusing to unbelievers of sound mind (1 Cor. 14:23).
4. Is the central part of worship in your local church "prophesying" as it ought to be and as it is in the churches of the saints (1 Cor. 14:24, 25), or is it "tongue speaking"?
5. We should worship in a church that characterizes the peace and stability of God our Father.

1 Cor. 14:34 | *Are Women to Keep Silence in Church?*

> *Let your women keep silence in the churches: for it is*
> *not permitted unto them to speak; but they are com-*
> *manded to be under obedience, as also saith the law.*

One question that we must resolve regarding this verse is whether the Apostle Paul was referring to women in general or to wives in particular.

Since the word *gunaíkes,* the plural of *gunē* (1135) can be translated as either "women" or "wives," we must choose the meaning that is most contextually plausible. In order to determine this, we must examine in this context whether the word *gunaíkes* relates to women in general or to wives in particular. In verse 35, Paul says, "And if they will learn anything, let them ask their own husbands at home. . . ." The word *ándras,* the accusative plural of *anēr* (435), can also have a dual meaning, that is, it can mean either a man or a husband. The translators have correctly rendered it as "husbands." But if *ándras* in verse 35 refers to husbands, then the noun *gunaíkes* in verse 34 must refer to wives. If *gunaíkes* were translated in verse 34 as "women" and *ándras* in verse 35 as "husbands," Paul would be seen as encouraging the indiscriminate cohabitation of women with men. Paul, however, who spent the whole chapter of 1 Corinthians 7 expounding on the sanctity of marriage, supported the monogamous marriage of one man and one woman, a husband and a wife. Therefore, if we translate the word *ándras* as "husbands" in verse 35, in order to be consistent, we must translate the noun *gunaíkes* as "wives" and not "women" in verse 34.

This command is not a prohibition against women speaking in the church simply because they are women. Paul, in Galatians 3:28, ascribes equality to the genders, but not uniformity. They are presented as two persons, male and female, a husband and a wife, forming one union, one body, and one soul; not with two separate heads, but one head over that one union. As in the Trinity (Matt. 28:19), God the Father and God the Son are two Persons, equal in essence (John 10:30), but having one head, so also in marriage a husband and wife are presented as having one head (1 Cor. 11:3). They are equal in essence as human beings, but having different personalities and functions.

The secret in understanding the relationship of three equal, eternal, and self-existent persons, God the Father, Son, and Holy Spirit (Matt. 28:19; Acts 5:3, 4), is the revelation of Jesus Christ in His incarnation. Christ as the unique Son (*monogenḗs* [3439]) was always in the bosom of the Father. John 1:18 uses the present participle *ho ṓn*, the One being, of the verb *eimí* (1510), to be, to express this eternal relationship of God the Father and God the Son. The exact translation of this present participle *ho ṓn* should not be "who is" or "which is" in the statement "the only begotten Son, who is in the bosom of the Father," but "who being in the bosom of the Father." The present participle would indicate that the Son, Christ in His eternity, has always been in the bosom of the Father, which expresses eternal and intimate relationship. The word for "declared" in John 1:18 is *exēgḗsato*, the third person singular aorist middle deponent indicative of *exēgéomai* (1834) derived from *ek* (1837), "out," and the verb *hēgéomai* (2233), to explain, lead out or forward. The compound verb means to lead out or to declare forth or tell

ARE WOMEN TO KEEP SILENCE IN CHURCH?

clearly the meaning of something. In John 1:1, 14, we are told that the eternal Word, *ho Lógos* (3056), the Logic, the Intelligence, became flesh. He became a tangible, discernible human being who dwelt among us. This human being, Jesus Christ, came from the bosom of the Father to earth to reveal to us who God the Father is.

First Corinthians 11:3 tells us that the head of Christ is God the Father. No one who was inferior to the Father could reveal Him adequately. Jesus Christ proved that He was God incarnate by raising Himself (John 2:19) from the dead, which no one has ever done before or since. He became flesh in order to shed His blood for the remission of our sins and to explain to us the mystery of the Godhead (*Theótēs* [2320]). Thus Jesus Christ became the interpretation of the mystery of God or the Godhead, which He could not be had He not always been part of the Trinity.

In John 1:1–18, the eternal Christ is called *ho Lógos* which not only means speech, but also intelligence. But we must bear in mind that besides the word *Lógos* which means Word and at the same time, intelligence, we have another Greek word which is expressive only of speech, and that is *laliá* (2981), speech. It is most significant that when reference is made to the incarnation of the Son of God, the word *Lógos* is used in John 1:1 and not *laliá*. The verb derived from this noun is *laléō* (2980), which means only to speak and is the word that is used in relation to speaking in a tongue or tongues in Corinth (1 Cor. 12:3, 30; 13:1, 11; 14:2–6, 9, 11, 13, 18–19, 21, 23, 27–29, 34–35, 39). Whereas the noun *laliá* (2981) means speech, it never means intelligence which expresses itself in speech as does the word *lógos*. The Lord Jesus is never called the *laliá*, the speech of God, but *ho Lógos*, the Word which presupposes intelligence. He is the Intelligence which became flesh; a spiritual personality became a physical entity. In becoming man, He could express Himself (John 1:1, 14) in a human, understandable language about His own eternal coexistence with the Father (John 1:18).

ARE WOMEN TO KEEP SILENCE IN CHURCH?

In a marriage which God brings about, He unites two persons, a male and a female, into one. As one united body and soul, they have one head which speaks in the united spirit or soul. That is the picture of Christian marriage which the Lord Jesus describes in Matthew 19:3–7 and Mark 10:1–12. It is the union that Paul explains in 1 Corinthians 11:3. It is also a similitude of the Church as the bride of Christ (Eph. 5:32).

Women in the Temple and the Synagogues

The place where Jews assembled to worship God was the temple which had different courtyards where they could sing songs and pray. Women were so important that there was a courtyard which was exclusively dedicated to them and may have been the largest space provided in the temple.

The institution that arose for corporate worship, in addition to the temple that included men and women, was the synagogue. The Greek word for "synagogue" is *sunagōgḗ* (4864) which comes from the conjunction *sún* (4862), together, denoting united purpose, and the verb *ágō* (71), to lead or bring. A synagogue was a place for gathering together individuals for one same purpose, to worship God. The oldest synagogue on record was the one built in Alexandria during the reign of Ptolemy the Third. Damascus had a number of synagogues in which Paul and the apostles preached (Acts 9:2, 20). Throughout Asia Minor and Greece, the islands, and in cities such as Ephesus, Philippi, Thessalonica, Berea, Athens, and Corinth, the synagogues were gathering places for Jews and God-fearing proselytes (Acts 13:14, 26, 33; 17:17) in which they offered a sphere of activity of corporate worship (Acts 14:1; 17:1, 17; 18:4, 7). In Rome, there were quite a number of synagogues at the time of Augustus.

Paul was a Jew who had always worshiped God in a synagogue. At the outset, the synagogue was a place of public instruction. At an early time, elementary schools for the young were established in them or nearby. There were additional uses for the synagogue other than the worship of God.

The traditional seating arrangement for the women in the synagogue was separate from the men. The divider sometimes was some form of a wall or barrier. In some places the balcony was reserved for the women. Thus the husbands and wives did not sit together as they do in the church services of our modern society. They sat separately, often at a distance, as they still do in many of the countries of the world. As women wanted to be adequately taught and the seating arrangement interfered with their hearing, the necessity of asking questions arose. But seated separately from their husbands, and sometimes at a distance, they would have to call to their husbands to ask questions. It seems that this custom was carried over to the Christian church. Paul thought that this procedure of learning was not good because it contributed to the confusion of voices already present by those who claimed they should speak because they were filled by the Holy Spirit. Never lose sight of the fact that speaking in languages other than one's own in an orderly manner resulted from the baptism of the Holy Spirit (see Acts 2:1–12), whereas the practice of the ecstatic outbursts of the unknown tongue was a disorderly practice in Corinth.

Paul did not wish to suppress the desire of the women to learn, but he wanted it to be orderly. He laid down the rule that wives should ask questions of their husbands at home and not in church, since the matter brought about noise and confusion in worship (v. 35). Thus historical and cultural explanations of conditions as they then existed explains why verse 35 says, "If they will learn anything, let them ask their husbands at home: for it is a shame for women to speak in the church."

ARE WOMEN TO KEEP SILENCE IN CHURCH?

"Let Your Women [Wives] Keep Silence"

In the King James Version, translating from the Textus Receptus, it says, "Let your women [wives] keep silence in the churches." The "your" (*humốn* [5216], your own) is not in the Nestle's Text from which the New American Standard Version is translated, nor is it in the United Bible Society text (Kurt Aland). The Textus Receptus, however, and the Majority Text have "your women [wives]." That is one more reason for translating *gunaíkes* as "wives" instead of "women." Clearly it is the Textus Receptus and the Majority Text that are preferred here.

Furthermore, there is the definite article *hai*, the feminine plural of *ho* (3588), the. Paul is not speaking here of women in general, but of the women who are the wives of particular men. This involves the responsibility and leadership of each Christian husband for his wife.

Paul was advising husbands to encourage their wives to keep calm and not participate in the terrible confusion that was taking place. They were to be advised not to disturb the sanctity of the worship service or carry on in ecstasy in imitation of the heathen priestesses of Delphi.

Just recently, I spoke in a church where one lady shouted out in ecstasy for about fifteen minutes until she finally fell on the floor in exhaustion and had to be revived. I cannot see how this could possibly be considered order and peace. It is such displays of uncontrolled behavior that Paul forbids.

"In the Churches"

Our verse then speaks of the area where this responsibility and leadership ought to be exercised, that is, "in the churches" referring to the local assemblies. In other words the husband was responsible for his family's behavior in church. He was wrong in abdicating his responsibility for the teaching of his spouse and the discipline of his children. This is not any different than it ought to be in the church today. If the responsibility is to be attributed to an individual, it ought to be presupposed by the leadership that one is meant to exercise. In our age, most men have abdicated the responsibility and discipline of the family to the wife. The purpose of this leadership responsibility was to maintain proper order so that those in the worship service may understand that God is not a God of confusion, but of peace and order. Thus the worshipers might concentrate and learn in a conducive atmosphere.

The tradition of the women sitting together, separate from their husbands was a tradition from the temple times and the synagogue gatherings. The Christian church later changed that, and rightly so since men and women are equal in God's sight.

You can imagine when you read 1 Corinthians 14 what a place of turmoil and noise the assembly of believers in Corinth was. It was so noisy and confusing that unbelievers would think that people who participated in the Christian worship services were mad, or were maniacs (*maínesthe* [3105]), as the Greek word has it (v. 23). The women sitting separately from their husbands would shout that they could not hear or disagreed with what they heard and would join in the tumult. It is no wonder that the Apostle Paul says *sigátōsan*, "Let them keep quiet [or 'hush,' the third person plural present active imperative of *sigáō* {4601} with the noun being *sigḗ* {4602}, silence]." This was tantamount to saying, Let them keep the prevailing order as in the other churches of the saints. The imperative is in the present tense which means that they were to stop shouting in the assembly. If the wives were to observe silence and not speak at all during the worship service, they would not be allowed to sing because singing is speaking melodiously. Nowhere do we find the Apostle Paul forbidding women to sing (Eph. 5:19; Col. 3:16).

Are Women to Keep Silence in Church?

Worship in the Corinthian Church

No one reading 1 Corinthians 14 would conclude that the worship in the Corinthian church was orderly and in good taste, as it was in all the other churches (v. 33).

There is no doubt that the worship in Corinth, according to 1 Corinthians 14:6–19, was so noisy that the clear message of the gospel did not get through. There seemed to be much noise, but no meaning to it. As Paul says in verse 11, "Therefore, if I know not the meaning of the voice, I shall be unto him that speaks a barbarian [one who speaks in his own language and does not care whether or not he is understood], and he that speaks shall be a barbarian unto me." Paul compared attendance in the church in Corinth as being among uncivilized people uneducated and unrefined, each one saying whatever entered his mind without regard to others. The mind remained uninstructed because no control or discipline was exercised. Paul says that he is not criticizing the Corinthian worship because of lack of education on his part. In fact, in verse 18, he says, "I thank my God, I speak with tongues [languages] more than you all." Paul was an exceptionally well-educated and brilliant person, but he did not flaunt this for self-aggrandizement. The Corinthian worship service must have seemed like a madhouse for Paul to say in verse 19, "Yet in the church I had rather speak five words with my understanding, that by my voice I might teach others also, than ten thousand words in an unknown tongue."

The result of the genuine baptism in the Holy Spirit in Acts 2:6, 7 was that they spoke in understandable languages other than their mother tongue. God, who is the dispenser of the gifts of the Holy Spirit (1 Cor. 12:4–11), is the God of intelligence and meaningful words, not confusion. The phenomenon of tongue-speaking in Corinth brought added confusion because the uninstructed (*idiṓtai* [2399]; see 1 Cor. 14:16, 23, 24) believed that it actually was the result of the Holy Spirit.

In addition to imitating the oracles of Delphi, the Corinthians were attempting to imitate Pentecost, which was indeed a phenomenon of the Holy Spirit. Thus we shall do well to examine the words "utterance" and "said" and their true meaning found in Acts 2:4, 14. Both of these words are translations of the verb *apophthéggomai* (669) which means the articulation of distinct words so that they have meaning to the listener. It is a compound verb from the preposition *apó* (575), from, or away from one's self, and *phthéggomai* (5350), meaning to articulate the voice and form meaningful sounds as contrasted to the noises of animals. *Phthóggos* (5353), sound, is spoken of distinguishable sounds so that one can know what a person has spoken or what a musical instrument is playing. A differentiation can be seen between the noun *laliá* talk (from the verb *laléō),* and *lógos,* the expression of the mind. The verb *apophthéggomai,* to articulate, is closer to *lógos* than to *laliá.*

The verb *apophthéggomai,* to articulate, is used only three times in the New Testament. Two of the times are related to Pentecost in Acts 2:4, 14. In verse 4 we read, "And they were all filled with the Holy Ghost, and began to speak with other tongues [languages], as the Spirit gave them utterance [*apophthéggesthai,* the present middle passive deponent infinitive of *apophthéggomai,* to articulate in a clear, understandable language]." On the other hand, in 1 Corinthians 14:8 when the noise of the unknown tongue is mentioned, it is compared to the uncertain sound (*ádēlon* [82], indistinct) of the trumpet, having no meaning. In verse 9, *apophthéggomai* of Acts 2:4, 14 is likened to a clear, distinguishable word. The expression used is *eúsēmon lógon. Eúsēmon* (2154) is derived from the adjective *eu* (2095), good, and *sēma* (n.f.), akin to *sēmeíon,* a sign, token; and *lógon,* a word that implies intelligent speaking. The adjective means well expressed, significant, of good omen, and is distinguishable by certain marks such as meaningful speech in which case it means that which is easily understood or distinct. Whereas speaking in an unknown tongue carried no significant word to the listener, the word given by the Holy Spirit was clear and meaningful.

In Acts 2:14 we read, "But Peter, standing up with the eleven, lifted up his voice and said unto them, 'You men of Judea, and all you that dwell at Jerusalem, be this known unto you, and hearken to my words.'" The word "said," referring to the preaching of Peter, is translated from the word *apephthégxato*, the third person singular aorist middle deponent indicative of *apophthéggomai*, which means that it was clearly spoken or articulated in a language to which one could understand and respond.

We find the third instance in Acts 26:25 where, in answering Festus, the Apostle Paul said, "I am not mad, most noble Festus; but speak forth [*apophthéggomai*] the words of truth and soberness [*sōphrosúnēs* {4997}, sound mind]." The Holy Spirit enables those whom He fills to enunciate clearly, understandably, meaningfully, and not foolishly as was the case in Corinth.

"For It Is Not Permitted to Them"

This command is given with the absolute "not" (*ou* [3756]). The Majority Text and Textus Receptus, from which the King James Version has been translated, have the verb *epitétraptai*, the third person singular perfect passive indicative of *epitrépō* (2010), to permit, to allow, of which the accurate translation would be, "it has not been permitted." The Nestle and UBS texts have it in the present passive indicative *epitrépetai*, which would translate "it is not permitted."

But who does not permit the women or wives to speak? In 1 Timothy 2:12, Paul does not say that it is not permitted or it has not been permitted, but "I do not permit [*ouk*, the absolute 'not'; *epitrépō*, I permit] a woman [a wife] to teach nor to usurp authority [*authenteín* {831}, to domineer] over [her] husband [*andrós*, the genitive of *anḗr*, man or husband which here should have been translated 'husband'], but to be in quietness [*hēsuchía* {2271}, quietness or tranquility, not 'silence' as some translators have it]" (a.t.). We shall come back to this separately as we do a thorough exegesis. We only mention it at this time to point out that in 1 Corinthians 14:34 the Apostle Paul says, "It has not been permitted," whereas 1 Timothy 2:12 says, "I do not permit."

"To Speak"

Before we can determine who is responsible for the prohibition against women (wives) speaking in church, however, we must ascertain what Paul means when he uses the verb "to speak" (*laleín*, the present active infinitive of *laléō*, to speak).

In the Greek New Testament, there are several verbs which are translated "speak." They are *légō* (3004), to say; *laléō* (2980), to speak; *eréō* (2046) and *homiléō* (3656), to discourse; and *phēmi* (5346), to make one's thoughts known, to speak or say, from which the words "prophet" (*prophḗtēs* [4396]) and "prophesy" *prophēteúō* [4395]) are derived. The verb that is preeminent in the discussion of speaking in languages other than one's own tongue and speaking in an unknown tongue, as the Corinthians did, is *laléō*, or the contracted *laló*. This is the same verb that is used in association with "tongues" or "tongue" in many other references (Mark 16:17; Acts 2:4, 11; 10:46; 19:6; 1 Cor. 12:30; 13:1; 14:2, 4–6, 13, 18–19, 23, 27–29, 34, 35, 39). One of its meanings as given in Kittell's *Theological Dictionary of the New Testament*, abridged in one volume by Geoffrey W. Bromiley, is the meaning "to prattle" or "to babble." It is also used for the sounds of animals and out-of-tune musical instruments. In regard to speech, it may denote sound rather than meaning in addition to the ability to speak. In this context, however, the meaning is "to prattle" (p. 506). In 1 Corinthians 14, the verb *laléō* occurs a total of twenty-four times. Here in 1 Corinthians 14:34, since it occurs in the discussion of the practice in Corinth of speaking in an unknown tongue which is vigorously condemned by the Apostle Paul, *laleín*, the present active infinitive of *laléō*, does not seem to refer here to intelligent speaking, but has the particular and predominant meaning of prattling or babbling. Paul, therefore, is not saying that *légein*, intelligent speaking, is forbidden, but *laleín*, prattling. *Légein*, or any of the other verbs meaning intelligent speaking, is not forbidden. In the same way that such prattling is forbidden for women, it is also forbidden for men to speak if there is no interpreter to give the meaning of what is said (1 Cor. 14:5, 13, 27). When one speaks, he should not be speaking into the air (v. 9) which he would be if no one understood what was said. Thus, the discrimination is not against women per se, but against senseless babbling for both men and women.

"But to Be Submissive"

It is necessary that we study carefully the most important word *hupotássesthai*, the present middle infinitive of *hupotássō* (5293), to subjugate, to cause to submit. In the middle voice, *hupotássomai* means to submit oneself voluntarily. In the King James translation, it is rendered, "But they are commanded to be under obedience." The New International Version says, "But must be in submission," and the Revised Standard Version says, "But should be subordinate."

These various translations bring us to two Greek words used in the New Testament that we should examine. The first one is the verb *hupakoúō* (5219), to obey. It is derived from the preposition *hupó* (5259), under, and the basic verb *akoúō* (191), to hear, to heed. As a compound verb, it means to heed and obey. The noun is *hupakoḗ* (5218), obedience. In the New Testament we find that the wife is never instructed to obey her husband. The word *hupakoúō* is never used in the relationship between a wife and her husband.

In Matthew 8:27, we read that the winds and the sea obeyed Jesus who commanded them to be still (cf. Mark 4:39; Luke 8:24). This was absolute obedience without thought or volition.

In Mark 1:27, we read, "for with authority commanded He even the unclean spirits, and they do obey Him [*hupakoúousin*, the third person present indicative of *hupakoúō*]." We see, therefore, that in addition to the disturbed sea, the unclean spirits or the demons involuntarily obeyed Jesus. He did not afford them the opportunity to disobey. The Lord exercised His omnipotence over the elements and the unclean spirits and they had no choice but to obey Him. As long as a wife is not figuratively a bag of uncontrolled wind or possessed by demons, she does not deserve to be treated as such. Nor is the husband to be treated similarly by his wife or by any fellow human being.

In Ephesians 6:1 and Colossians 3:20, children, on the other hand, are commanded to obey their parents because, due to their young age, they are unable to exercise mature and wise judgment. "Children obey [*hupakoúete*] your parents in the Lord: for this is right." Colossians 3:20 says, "For this is well pleasing unto the Lord." This is equivalent to "the law" of 1 Corinthians 14:34. Just as children are to obey their parents, so servants are commanded to obey their masters. In Ephesians 6:5, Paul says, "Servants [*doúloi* {1401}, slaves who are not allowed to exercise any will of their own] be obedient [*hupakoúete*] to them that are your masters according to the flesh" (cf. Col. 3:22).

The verb, however, which is used in 1 Corinthians 14:34 is *hupotássomai*, the middle voice of *hupotássō* (5293), to arrange under, derived from the preposition *hupó*, under, and the verb *tássō* (5021), to place in order. The middle voice means that the wife voluntarily places herself under her husband in the proper order instituted by God. It is not forced upon her. Again, it is God's arrangement which, if kept properly, provides peace and order. From the verb *tássō* comes the noun *táxis* (5010), order, arrangement (1 Cor. 14:40). The derivatives of the verb *tássō* are: *anatássomai* (392), to compose in an orderly manner; *antitássō* (498), to resist; *apotássō* (657), to set in its proper category away from oneself; *átaktos* (813), disorderly, irregular; *diatássō* (1299), set in order, issue orderly and detailed instructions; *epitássō* (2004), to order; *prostássō* (4367), a specific command for a specific person; *protássō* (4384), to foreordain; *suntássō* (4929), to arrange or set in order together; *tágma* (5001), an order, regular method; *taktós* (5002), arranged, appointed; *táxis* (5010), an arrangement; *hupotássō* (5293), to place under. God has created and designed things that each may fit in the totality of creation in perfect order. A child goes to the class for which he is mentally fitted according to his age and development. This is called *táxis*, the proper class or place where he fits intellectually.

In marriage, which is the Apostle Paul's concern in our study, there are two people involved, a husband and a wife, and each should understand his or her position in order to please God who has fitted them together. That there are two genders among humans is not something that has evolved but is God-designed. It is pleasing to God if the parties involved acknowledge that His design is proper and honorable, and consequently will abide by it and thus reap His blessings. To symbolize that proper fitting together, the Apostle Paul has chosen Christ and his Church (Eph. 5:32). The purpose for which Paul gave this allegory of the Church being the wife of Christ is to impress upon us how unconditional the love of the husband toward his wife should be. A wife should be loved as Christ loves the Church—with a love that is continuous and undiminished. In verse 33 Paul said, "Nevertheless, let every one of you in particular so love his own [*heautoú* {1438}] wife even as himself; and the wife see that she reverence her husband."

The conclusion of the matter is that when the husband loves his wife as Christ loves His Church, there will be no difficulty at all with the wife submitting herself to the loving protection and care of her husband. This is Christian marriage as it ought to be.

As in 1 Corinthians 14:34, in 1 Timothy 2:8–15 Paul speaks about wives and husbands, not women and men. In studying this passage we see one word occurring which can be translated as either "men" or "husbands" (*ándres*), and one word that can be translated as either "women" or "wives" (*gunaíkes*). There is a word in verse 4 that includes both men and women, husbands and wives, and that is the generic word *ánthrōpoi*, the plural of *ánthrōpos* (444), a human being. In this verse Paul says that Christ would rather be God and Savior of all men, that is, both men and women: "Who will have all men [*anthrōpous*] to be saved, and to come unto the knowledge of the truth."

In verses 8 and 9, however, Paul speaks of men who, through Christian marriage, become husbands, and women who become wives. He does not make a distinction favoring one against the other when it comes to the privilege of prayer which is our free access into the presence of God (Rom. 5:2; Eph. 2:18; 3:12).

First Timothy 2:8 says, "I will [*boúlomai* {1014}, desire] therefore that men [*ándras*, men or husbands] pray everywhere, lifting up holy hands without wrath and doubting." These conditions for praying in any place, including the church, are that those hands that are lifted to heaven in supplication must be "sacred [*hósioi* {3741}, thus pure] hands." For the husband to be holy and thus able to "lift up holy hands," he must obey the word of God and love his wife as Christ loves the Church.

Verse 9 begins with the adverb "likewise" or "in the same manner" (*hōsaútōs* [5615], also; *kaí* [2532], and, also, implying as it is with men or husbands, so also with the women or wives). Here the verb *proseúchesthai,* the present middle deponent infinitive of *proseúchomai* (4336), to pray, is implied although not repeated. So private and public prayer is not only the privilege of men, but of women and wives, as is clearly stated in 1 Corinthians 11:4, 5.

First Timothy 2:9, 10 also includes the women's dress. Paul adds this detail because public prayer was included. And then follows the preposition *en* (1722), in, indicating how women should be dressed while participating in public prayer. With the verb, "pray" understood, these verses should read:

> [to pray publicly] dressed in a long garment [the dative singular feminine noun *katastolḗ* {2689}, a long garment or robe] that is decent [*kosmíō,* the dative of *kósmios* {2887}, decent but at the same time beautiful] with shamefacedness [*metá* {3326}, with; *aidoús,* the genitive of *aidṓs* {127}, an inner sense of what is right and proper and does not bring shame] and sober mindedness [*sōphrosúnēs,* the genitive of *sōphrosúnē* {4997}, a saved mind, from *sóos* {n.f. in NT}, saved, and *phrónēsis* {5428}, prudence, mindset, that which guides a Christian in interpersonal relations], to adorn [*kosmeín,* the present infinitive of *kosméō* {2885}, to adorn, with which the adjective *kósmios* used previously is related] themselves, not with braided hair or gold or pearls or costly clothing; but which [implying clothing] becomes women professing godliness, with [*diá* {1223}] good works.

There is no doubt that Paul is speaking here about Christian women. Having told us that when a woman prays in public, she should be dressed decently with a sense of what is right and proper but not extravagantly, he now tells us in verse 11 what her inner attitude should be. First of all, she should be teachable or willing to learn (*manthanétō* [3129]). Secondly, in order to be teachable, she should be calm and composed (*hēsuchía* [2271]), and thirdly, she ought to be submissive (*hupotagé* [5292]).

We cannot but connect 1 Corinthians 14:34, 35 with 1 Timothy 2:11. In 1 Corinthians 14:34 Paul says, "Your [TR; MT] wives, let them keep quiet [calm {*sigátōsan*}] in the churches." For with the verb "let them keep quiet [*sigátōsan*]," Paul uses the expression *sigátōsan* from *sigáō*, "while in 1 Timothy 2:11 he uses the expression "Let the women learn [*manthanétō*] in silence [*hēsuchía* {2271}, quietness]." She certainly should be allowed to learn, but she should take care that her learning may not create more commotion than already exists. This was in view of the great noise that was made by those speaking in tongues. Paul was urging them not to add to the confusion of the Corinthian worship service.

Timothy was not a stranger to the problems that existed in Corinth, for he knew that the Corinthians were very emotional in their worship. The Second Epistle to the Corinthians begins, "Paul, an apostle of Jesus Christ by the will of God, and Timothy our brother." To be persuaded of this, one does not have to do anything else but read 1 Corinthians 14 and particularly verse 14, for Timothy was sent by Paul to Corinth to correct the situation of ecstatic behavior during their worship service (1 Cor. 4:17).

The commandment and advice contained in 1 Timothy 2:11, 12 pertains to the situation prevailing in and peculiar to the worship of the Corinthian church. This we can safely deduce from the fact that only in these verses and in 1 Corinthians 14:34 is such advice found. Since Timothy was sent by the Apostle Paul to resolve the problem, he now alludes to it. One way to do so was to encourage husbands to assume their responsibility to see to it that their wives were submissive to the law and order of the worship service (1 Cor. 11:13). Thus Paul writes in

1 Timothy 2:11, "Let the woman [wife] learn [*manthanétō*, the third person singular present active imperative of *manthánō*, to learn] in silence with all submission." The verb is the same as in 1 Corinthians 14:35: "And if they would learn anything, let them ask their husbands at home." The verb "learn" is *mathein*, the second aorist active infinitive of *manthánō*, to learn, which indicates that there was something in particular that the wives wanted to ask their husbands. There is an intimacy attached to the verb *manthánō*, to learn, since the word *mathētés* (3101), disciple, comes from it. The followers of Jesus were His disciples (Matt. 8:21; Luke 6:13, 17; 7:11; John 6:60, 66). *Manthánō* implies not only learning, but a closeness of relationship which certainly exists between a husband and wife. There are certain matters which can only be discussed between them.

"As Also Says the Law"

Nowhere in the Law of Moses is it written that women are not allowed to speak. What law is it, therefore, that prohibits such speaking by women? Paul does not delineate the law to which he is referring. We believe that it is the law of order, instituted by God Himself who is a God of peace and not of confusion. This, however, would apply to both men and women. The word *nómos* (3551) usually has an adjunct which designates the giver of the law, as the Law of Moses (John 1:17; 7:19, etc.). Notice that the verb used in the phrase "as even the law says" is not *lalei*, which is the predominant verb used in speaking with tongues or in a tongue, but the verb *légei*, the third person singular of *légō* (3004), meaning to speak.

A distinction must be made between the speaking in an unknown tongue and the prophetic ability to speak in languages other than one's own native tongue for the benefit of those who understand. We find this promise in Mark 16:17. The exact translation of this verse is, "And these signs shall follow the ones who believe; in My name shall they cast out demons; they shall speak in new [*kainaís,* the dative plural feminine adjective of *kainós* {2537}, qualitatively new] languages." Note that the promise was not for the Corinthian ecstatic tongue which the King James translators have rendered as "an unknown tongue."

We find that the qualitatively new languages were spoken miraculously, without having been learned by the individuals concerned during the apostolic age. These were definite ethnic languages. Those who practice what they believe to be the Corinthian gift of speaking in an unknown tongue, or in ecstasy, are unable to speak in ethnic languages which they have not learned.

At Pentecost Foreign Languages Were Spoken

We find, however, that on the day of Pentecost those who were assembled together in Jerusalem spoke in other languages. Acts 2:4 says, "And all were filled with the Holy Spirit, and began speaking in other [*hetérais,* the dative plural feminine adjective of *héteros* {2087}, other than one's own] languages [*glóssais,* dative plural feminine noun of *glóssa* {1100}, language or tongue] as the Spirit was giving [*edídou,* third person singular imperfect active indicative of *dídōmi* {1325} to give] them utterance." "The Spirit" here is the Holy Spirit. We must note that the imperfect tense implies temporary but continuous use at the time of giving. The phrase "was giving utterance" is *apophthéggesthai,* (present middle deponent infinitive of *apophthéggomai* [669]) and means the formation of sounds that corresponded to the comprehensible conveyance of meaning as the others who were present heard them. These languages stand in contrast to incomprehensible sounds. This was indeed a product of the Holy Spirit. It enabled believers gathered in Jerusalem to speak ethnic languages which they did not know to strangers from many countries who were gathered there.

Are Women to Keep Silence in Church?

That these were ethnic languages or dialects there is no doubt because in verses 6 and 8 we have the word "dialect" (*diálektos* [1258]) meaning the specific language of a county. This is the noun of the verb *dialégomai* (1256) which means to converse, and which verb in the active voice means to choose to speak in a specific language. One chooses to speak the language that the person with whom he is speaking understands. When I speak to someone, my mind tells me to choose the language that this person will best understand.

Women Also Spoke in Foreign Languages at Pentecost

Now, who were gathered together in that upper room in Jerusalem when the Holy Spirit filled them and they were enabled to speak in languages other than their own native tongues? Acts 1:14 tells us: "These all continued with one accord in prayer and supplication, with the women, and Mary the mother of Jesus, and with his brethren." Notice that there were women present, and especially a distinguished and honored woman, Mary the mother of Jesus. Now notice what Acts 2:4 says, "They were all [*hápantes,* the nominative plural masculine adjective of *hápas* {537}, all in a group] filled with the Holy Spirit and began [the subject of the verb continues to be all in the group] to speak in other languages [other than their own] as the Holy Spirit was giving them utterance." The women present were not excluded from participation in the miraculous events in Jerusalem on the day of Pentecost. Certainly the mother of Jesus was not excluded.

Acts 2:11 is also significant for us to note. "Cretans and Arabs we do hear them speaking in our own languages the wonderful works of God." The language of the Cretans was Greek and the language of the Arabs was Arabic. These were ethnic languages or dialects which they were able to speak as a result of the Holy Spirit's filling. Evidence of the Spirits' work abounded as those who heard them speak understood the languages they used. This took place during the event of Pentecost as the imperfect *edídou* (was giving) implies.

Evidently those assembled in Jerusalem upon whom the Holy Spirit came were all Jews (Acts 2:5), but Jesus Christ did not come into the world to save Jews only, but also Gentiles, and from them both to form the Church of God (1 Cor. 10:32). Chapters 10 and 11 of Acts speak of the coming of the Holy Spirit upon Gentiles, of whom the leading figure was Cornelius. It was in Caesarea that Peter in his sermon said, "Of a truth I perceive that God is no respecter of persons" (Acts 10:34). In Acts 11:15, Peter, a Jew, said, "As I began to speak, the Holy Ghost fell on them [the Gentiles] as on us at the beginning [at Pentecost]." And verse 16 says, "And I remembered the Word of the Lord, how that He said, 'John indeed baptized with water; but you shall be baptized with the Holy Ghost.'" And then in Acts 10:45, it says, "And they of the circumcision [the Jews] which believed were astonished, as many as came with Peter, because that on the Gentiles also was poured out the gift of the Holy Ghost." The Gentiles also experienced the result of the baptism in the Holy Spirit: "For they heard them speak with tongues [*glōssais*, languages other than their own], and magnify God" (v. 46). They understood what they were saying.

At Ephesus They Were Disciples of John the Baptist

The same thing happened with the Ephesian disciples of John in Acts 19:1–7. They, too, on being baptized by the Holy Spirit of which they had not heard previously, spoke with languages other than their own and prophesied (v. 6). Although they had not heard of the Holy Spirit, that did not hinder the Holy Spirit from activating faith in their hearts so that they could believe.

ARE WOMEN TO KEEP SILENCE IN CHURCH?

They Were All Baptized in the Holy Spirit, Not Simply Filled by the Holy Spirit

In all these historic instances, when the people concerned were baptized in the Holy Spirit, they spoke in languages other than their own as a sign of their identification with Christ in the baptism of the Holy Spirit (Matt. 3:11; Mark 1:8; Luke 3:16; John 1:33; Acts 1:5; 11:16; 1 Cor. 12:13). In each instance, there was an apostle present and it was only a temporary manifestation and not a permanent acquisition of miraculously being able to speak a new language. We never find any of the people who were baptized in the Holy Spirit having been endowed with the permanent ability to speak one or more foreign languages which they had not learned cognitively. Nor does Scripture record that anyone was enabled to speak another language miraculously and permanently as a result of the empowerment of the Holy Spirit. That some people have a gift of learning languages is evident, and it is not uncommon for a person to speak five or six languages. However, this takes time, diligence, and study.

The Phenomenon at Corinth

That which is described in 1 Corinthians 14:26–32, however, is characterized as a phenomenon of disorderly conduct, hence the necessity of Paul saying in verse 33 that God is not a God of confusion (*akatastasías*). Whenever the speaking was in a tongue (*glōssa* [singular]), it referred to the speaking in an unknown tongue and producing much confusion. Such is the case in verses 2 and 4, the subject also being singular. In verse 4, the contrast is given of the person who speaks in an unknown tongue as edifying only himself, but he who prophesies and his prophecy is understood, edifies the church. The only way that such behav-

ior can be tolerated is to have an interpretation of the unknown
tongue and no more than one speaking at a time (vv. 29–31).

In verse 6, Paul says, "If I come and speak in languages
that are unknown to you, what will I profit you?" What a person speaks ought to be understood, otherwise he would be
speaking into the air (vv. 7–9). Edification (v. 12), interpretation
(v. 13), and understanding (v. 15) must be the result. When
Paul says in verse 18, "I thank my God, I speak with tongues [or
languages other than my own] more than you all," he uses the
plural *glōssai* which means languages. The meaning of the plural
word for "tongues" or "languages" is ethnic languages or dialects, while the phenomenon that abounded in Corinth was an
ecstatic utterance called "a tongue" or, as the King James Version
properly renders it, "an unknown tongue." This is what was
bringing confusion to the Corinthian worship. Suppose a stranger
came into the church while everyone was speaking in strange
languages that were not interpreted and not understood, or
they were engaged in ecstatic utterances. We have just this situation described in verse 23: "If therefore the whole church
would come together in one place, and all speak with tongues
[uninterpreted languages], and there come in those that are
unlearned, or unbelievers, will they not say that you are mad
[maniacs which word derives from *maínesthe*, the second person
plural present middle deponent indicative of *maínomai* {3105},
to act as a maniac]?"

In Scripture we do not find this behavior in Christian worship in any church other than the church at Corinth. It is significant, then, that Paul closes this discussion of 1 Corinthians
14 with verse 33: "For God is not the author of confusion, but
of peace, as in all churches of the saints." No one reading
1 Corinthians would come to the conclusion that the worship in
the Corinthian church was orderly and in good taste, as it was
in all the other churches.

ARE WOMEN TO KEEP SILENCE IN CHURCH?

There is no doubt that the worship in Corinth, according to 1 Corinthians 14:6–19, was so noisy that the clear message of the gospel did not get through. There seemed to be much noise, but no meaning to it. As Paul says in verse 11, "Therefore, if I know not the meaning of the voice, I shall be unto him that speaks a barbarian [one who speaks in his language and does not care whether or not he is understood], and he that speaks shall be a barbarian unto me." Paul compared the church in Corinth as being among uncivilized people, each one saying whatever entered his mind in disregard of others. The mind remains uninstructed because no control nor discipline is exercised. Paul explains that he is not criticizing the Corinthian worship because of his own lack of education. In fact, in verse 18, he says, "I thank my God, I speak with tongues [languages] more than you all." Again, in contrast to the practice in the Corinthian worship services, these were learned languages.

LESSONS:

1. Paul does not speak about women in general in verse 34, but about wives.
2. He is advising husbands to guide their wives. He says "your wives" as verse 35 speaks of "their own husbands."
3. The verb *sigáō* (4601) does not mean to keep silence but to keep quiet as 1 Timothy 2:12 affirms with the noun *hēsuchía* (2271), quietness, tranquility (see Rev. 8:1 and the noun *sigḗ* [4602] derived from the verb *sigáō*). If *sigáō* meant speechlessness, then not only would speaking in church be out of order but also singing (1 Cor. 14:15).
4. The verb *laléō* (2980) here, and generally in 1 Corinthians 14, is used to refer to babble or chatter.
5. The verb *hupotássomai* (5293) refers to voluntary submissiveness in the relationship of a wife to her husband. This is because her husband loves her as his own body (Eph. 5:28). It does not refer to a woman in general being submissive to any man because that would attribute to Paul

the teaching of immorality. It is not the verb *hupakouō* (5219), obey, which is used and which implies unwilling obedience.

6. The law is God's order in creation and operation of the world and the sanctity of marriage.

ARE WOMEN TO KEEP SILENCE IN CHURCH?

1 Cor. 14:35 | *Questions Are to Be Discussed at Home*

And if they will learn anything, let them ask their husbands at home: for it is a shame for women to speak in the church.

One matter of concern dealt with in 1 Corinthians 14 is speaking in an unknown tongue or in a language that is not understood by the hearers. When it comes to the edification of others, it is better to prophesy (vv. 1, 24, 25). And when it comes to prophecy, not all should speak together, but one at a time with a maximum of three (v. 29). If one of the listeners wants to speak while another is speaking, he should wait until the other ceases to speak (v. 30). Order and decency should be the rule in both speaking and prophesying.

"And If"

Notice that the verse we are studying begins with the hypothetical conjunction *ei* (1487), if. "And if they will learn anything." The implication is that when questions arose, they should wait until they were at home where the discussion would not disturb others and where they would have far more freedom to speak about various matters. The intimacy of a wife and husband gives such freedom. This has nothing to do with intelligence, but that specific "something" (*ti*, the accusative singular neuter indefinite pronoun of *tis* [5100], something) the wife wants to know about.

"They Desire to Learn Something"

The aorist infinitive in which the verb *matheín*, learn, is found, indicates a specific matter in question. Whereas this tells us how a woman should learn from her husband, it also indicates that the general teaching process should be carried on in peace and quietness.

We should bear in mind that at that time usually only men received an education. The education of women was considered unnecessary, for the woman's task was to care for the family whereas the man was to provide for the family which was more likely to require mathematical and literary abilities. Consequently, it was common for women to be illiterate and indeed quite rare for a woman to be educated. Thus the wives had to depend on their husbands if they ever hoped to make progress in this area. This state of affairs is still extremely common in many parts of the world. We can only surmise a woman's confusion and frustration as she tried to understand the teaching of the Word of God. Question after question must have risen which she wanted answered, and Paul tells the Corinthians that this is a personal matter that should be done in the privacy and intimacy of the home, not in the public worship service. We all know also that one learns much better and quicker in a quiet and tranquil atmosphere.

"Let Them Ask Their Husbands at Home"

What is translated as "let them ask" in Greek is *eperōtátōsan*, the third person plural present active imperative of *eperōtáō* (1905), to interrogate, inquire. It is derived from the preposition *epí* (1909), upon, in addition to, concentrate on, and is used as an intensive; and *erōtáō* (2065), to ask, inquire of. This implies presumed or real equality between the subject asking and the one asked as of God the Father and the Lord Jesus Christ in John 14:16; 16:26; 17:9. It stands in contrast to the verb *aiteō* (154), request, which involved asking from an inferior to a superior (John 14:13, 14, 16:26).

It is to be noted that the wives are to ask of their own (*idíous* [2398], one's own) husband. They were not to ask just any of the men (*ándras* [435]) simply because they were men. In these two words, the verb *eperōtátōsan*, let them ask additionally, and the adjective *idíous*, their own, may lie the true exegesis of this extremely difficult verse.

The verb *eperōtáō*, to inquire, occurs fifty-four times in the Gospels, three times in the Acts, once in Romans, and once in the Corinthian epistles here in verse 35. Not only is it the single occurrence in the Corinthian epistles, but it occurs only in connection with a matter pertaining to a wife and her husband. And it seems that it may have been in reference to a particular matter that required privacy as the particle *ti* (5101), something, indicates. The Apostle Paul did not have confidence that the Corinthians would not publicly discuss in church some intimate matters which should be discussed at home in privacy. With Corinth being the cosmopolitan, sinful city that it was, there was even a characterization among the Greeks as "acting like a Corinthian" (*Korinthiázomai*) which meant to engage in sin and debauchery. There were those who entered the church worship service in Corinth whose temptation was to bring the Corinthian lifestyle into the church. Paul, desiring to stop the evil from spreading, instructs that such questioning be reserved for the privacy of the home. In 1 Corinthians 12:3 Paul reveals something strange which was happening among the Corinthians who were speaking in an unknown tongue. Apparently in the frenzy of their so doing, some of them were calling Jesus accursed: "For I make known to you, that no man speaking by the

Spirit of God calls Jesus accursed: and that no one can say that Jesus is the Lord, but by the Holy Spirit."

"At Home"

There is a contrast here which we must understand—"at home" and "at church." It is as if Paul wants to point out that there are some matters that ought to be discussed in public, in church, and some that should be discussed only at home.

"For It Is Shameful"

That the matter a wife asks her husband about is private is explicit in the adjective that is used in giving the reason for such inappropriateness. Paul says, "For it is shameful for women [the wives] to speak in the church." The Greek for the expression "it is a shame" is *aischrón esti* (*aischrón,* the nominative of the adjective *aischrós* [150], indecent, that which brings shame [*aischúnē*]; *estí* [2076], is). Let us examine three words which are related to the word "shame."

One can experience shame if he is caught in an act that is not accepted as moral and decent. That is called *aischúnē* (152). The accepted standard can be set by society or by God. It all depends on who regulates what is considered moral. For the believer in Christ, the standard is set in God's Word, the Bible. For instance, it is a shame and disgrace to be caught in an act of fornication, which term includes all kinds of immorality. The adjective that is used in our verse is related to the noun *aischúnē.*

The second Greek work is *entropḗ* (1791), introspection, meaning the innate withdrawal resulting from fear of exposure of wrongdoing. The verb is *entrépomai* (1788) from the preposition *en* (1722), in, and *trépomai,* to turn or turn inward, to be ashamed, but not because one's wrongdoing has been found out, but from the fear of being found out. From this we get our English word "trepidation." This noun is used only twice. In

1 Corinthians 6:5, we read "I speak to your shame [*entropén*]. Is it so, that there is not a wise man among you? No, not one that shall be able to judge between his brethren?" The same noun is also found in 1 Corinthians 15:34: "Awake to righteousness, and sin not; for some have not the knowledge of God: I speak this to your shame." If such were found to be so, the believers would experience shame (*aischúnē*). So that it might not result in shame, they should exercise introspection.

The third word is *aidōs* (127), modesty, an innate moral repugnance to a dishonorable act or passion. It is not the avoidance of something because it will bring shame if one is caught in the action or the sheer thought of the shame that it would bring if one perpetrated it, but refraining from wrongdoing because of moral or godly principles. In this passage of Scripture the King James Version translates the noun as "shamefacedness": "In like manner, that women adorn themselves in modest apparel with shamefacedness and sobriety." Other translations have rendered the word as "modesty" (RSV, NIV, NASB). In Hebrews 12:28 it is translated "reverence." One should acknowledge the indecency of a certain deed and not fall into its trap. It actually means out of a sense of moral decency and of divine precept.

"For Women [Wives]"

As the plural is used for husbands (*ándras*), similarly the plural is used in regard to wives (*gunaixín,* the dative plural feminine of *gunē,* [1135] woman or wife). The plural use of both nouns would lead us to believe that a common practice existed in the Corinthian church which distinguished itself as different from all the other churches of the saints (v. 33).

Also our suspicion that such indiscreet speech was a common practice in Corinth is strengthened by the fact that the verb *laleín,* the infinitive of the verb *laleō,* (2980) to speak, is in the present tense.

QUESTIONS ARE TO BE DISCUSSED AT HOME

Women and wives were not forbidden by Paul to speak in church if their message was meaningful and meant for the edification of the assembly (1 Cor. 11:5; 14:4, 19). The same applies to singing of songs by women (1 Cor. 14:15).

"To Speak in the Church"

The verb usually translated "to speak" is *laleín* (the present infinitive of *laléō*), the same as in verse 34. In the context of 1 Corinthians 14, *laléō* (2980) means to prattle or to babble. The Apostle Paul's concern was that the church services ought to be occasions for edification (*oikodomḗ* [3619]). It is noteworthy that the verb *laléō* occurs in different forms in verses 4, 5, 13, and 27, more than in any other chapter of the Bible. And the noun *oikodomḗ* occurs in 1 Corinthians 14:3, 5, 12, 26, again more than in any chapter of the New Testament. A church service is ideal for edification if all things are done decently and in order.

Regardless of gender, those who attend any church service are either believers or unbelievers. Believers will be edified if they hear the Word of God in their own language. As far as unbelievers are concerned, the only sensible way for them to hear the gospel is in their own language or in a language which they understand. In Paul's view, it makes no difference what that language is as long as it is understood by both believers and unbelievers who are present. In Acts 9:4–6 when the Lord spoke in His resurrection glory to Saul of Tarsus, He spoke to him in a language that he understood: "Saul, Saul, why do you persecute me?" That was heavenly speech, but it was understood by Saul, and because he understood it, his answer was, "Who are you, Lord?" And when the Lord told Saul, "I am Jesus whom you persecute: it is hard for you to kick against the pricks," Saul again understood what the Lord was saying. "And he, trembling and astonished, said, 'Lord, what will You have me to do?' and the Lord said unto him, 'Arise, and go into the city and it shall be told to you what you must do.'" Note that the phrase "it shall be told you" is the verb *lalēthēsetai*, the third person singular future passive indicative of *laleō*. This verb, which basically means "to speak," is used in a different context in 1 Corinthians 14:34, 35. The Lord told Saul that when he would receive instructions, he would understand them and that His grace would enable him to obey because it was irresistible.

Paul, however, as he ministered in Corinth, found a phenomenon that the Christians apparently imitated from nearby Delphi. This was a city at the slope of Mount Parnassus which had become the headquarters of the prophetic oracles of the mythological god Apollo. It was said that Apollo was the son of the chief of the mythological gods, the principal being Zeus, and his wife, Leto. He was a twin brother of Artemis (Diana) to whom a great temple was consecrated in Ephesus. The ancient Greeks and Romans believed that the mythological gods took a personal interest in their affairs, and they asked advice of these gods. The gods were supposed to answer by means of the oracles, but the people often were unable to understand the oracles for they were usually ambiguous. Because the answers were ambiguous, no one could accuse the gods of being wrong. However, special priests claimed to know what was meant and then told the people who in turn rewarded the priests with gifts. The temple where the answers were given was often called an "oracle." The most famous oracle of all was in Delphi in Greece, just across the Gulf of Corinth. Croesus, king of Lydia, consulted the gods before he invaded Cappadocia. The oracles said that if he invaded this country, he would bring ruin to an empire. They did not, however, specify which empire. Croesus thought this meant that he would win, but it was his own empire that was ruined. Many people pretended to be oracles, deceiving the worshipers and taking their money.

QUESTIONS ARE TO BE DISCUSSED AT HOME

It seems obvious that the influence of Delphi was felt across the gulf of Corinth. It is to be noted that Delphi gained importance as early as 1100 B.C., and it later became an international Greek shrine. The Pythian games in Delphi became prevalent, and it is to these Pythian games that Paul refers to in 1 Corinthians 9:24–27.

In Delphi there was a woman oracle or "prophetess" called Pythia who would utter weird sounds while in a frenzy. She was a peasant woman over fifty years old. After purifying herself in the Castalian Fountain and drinking of the water of the Kassoti and chewing a laurel leaf, she took her seat upon a tripod. This was placed over the chasm in the Adyton. Intoxicated by the exhalations from the chasm, she uttered incoherent sounds which were always obscure to the inquirer who usually returned home more mystified than he had come. People believed these were the words of the god Apollo. Temple priests interpreted these words to the public, and cities all over Greece, as well as private individuals, sought her advice. As a result, the oracle quickly influenced Greek religion, economics, and politics. The influence gradually waned in later Greek and Roman times. The Christian Roman emperor Theodosius closed the sanctuary in A.D. 390. Until that time, this heathen sanctuary was fully operative with the women playing a main role in the oracles. The reverberations of the Pythian oracles and the role of women undoubtedly had a profound influence upon nearby Corinth.

The interpretation of the difficult passages of the Corinthian epistle concerning the role of women in the church cannot be ignored as unrelated to the part women played in the oracle of Apollo. Apollo was, after all, not only the chief god of Delphi, but also of heathen Corinth. Even in Corinth today, the columns of Apollo's ancient temple remain outstanding. This mythological god had greatly influenced large cities like Ephesus and

Corinth. When Paul brought the gospel there, one of the first things he had to do was set forth God's law of the genders (Eph. 5:22–33). He reminded the Corinthians that God created both genders in His image (Gen. 1:27; 1 Cor. 11:3–15; Gal. 3:28), and he was aware of the unique way God had created woman out of one of Adam's ribs (Gen. 2:21–23). This is why he speaks of the man as the head of the woman, and that the man is not out of the woman, but the woman is out of the man, and that the man was not created for the woman, but the woman for the man (1 Cor. 11:3, 8, 9).

Paul did not want the Corinthian church to be copying the sanctuary of Apollo which constituted the heathen gathering for worship. In heathen worship in Delphi, and most probably in Corinth, the women predominated in speaking for Apollo.

Paul had to overcome this influence that existed in Corinth from Delphi just across the gulf of Corinth, and he wrote to Timothy regarding the problems that existed there because he was involved in the ministry of the Corinthian church (1 Cor. 4:17; 16:10, 11). He tells the Corinthians that the role of a Christian woman should not be the same as the role of a woman in heathen temples. It should not be thus in the Christian church by either men or women. There should be order in the church as there is in a marriage sanctified by Christ.

The woman a man chooses to be his companion for life reveals his character. In 1 Corinthians 11:7 she is called his "glory." The word "glory" is *dóxa* (1391) which comes from the verb *dokéō* (1380), to recognize, think. By living a godly and pure life, a wife brings honor to her husband. If she is dressed decently, it reveals the husband's decency in his choice of a wife (1 Tim. 2:9, 10). The life and behavior of all Christians should bring glory and honor to their Lord. Does yours?

LESSONS:

1. The word translated "women" should be rendered "wives" in the phrase "for it is shameful for wives to speak in church."

2. Since a wife depicts her husband's standards, she should be the concern of her husband.

3. Paul's concern is that the sanctity of marriage should be preserved and demonstrated as a union with one head, that of the husband.

4. This verse should be studied in conjunction with 1 Timothy 2:8–12 where Paul says that he personally does not permit what is not permitted by God's law of order and decency.

5. The verb "to speak" is *laleō* (2980) here and in 1 Corinthians 14:34 with the particular meaning of "chatter, prattle, babble."

6. A believer's behavior reflects on his Lord. Have you examined your behavior lately to see if you are an honorable member of Christ's body?

Questions Are to Be Discussed at Home

1 Cor. 14:36	*God's Word Is Settled and Unchangeable*

Or came out the Word of God from you? or came it unto you only?

Paul wanted the Corinthian church to realize that their form of worship gave the idea that God is a God of confusion and not of peace and order, which impression was not conveyed in the other churches: "For God is not the author of confusion, but of peace, as in all churches of the saints" (v. 33). God is immutable and not a God of continuing revelation in a state of change. His Word was once delivered unto the saints and cannot be added to nor subtracted from. (See Jude 3; Rev. 22:18, 19.) The Corinthians did not realize that "Forever, O Lord, Your Word is settled in heaven" (Ps. 119:89). They thought that they could add to God's revealed Word by receiving direct revelations from the Spirit of God. Thus Paul hesitated to call the Corinthians "spiritual" (*pneumatikoi* [4152], 1 Cor. 3:1).

The adjective "spiritual" (*pneumatikós*) has the noun *pneúma* (4151), spirit, in it. In defining God, the true God, whom our Lord came to reveal, Jesus said that He is Spirit (John 4:24). This essential characteristic of deity, however, is likely to be misunderstood as lacking permanence and solidity. In speaking to Nicodemus, the Lord Jesus spoke of the Spirit of God as coming from above (John 3:3, 7). He meant that the Spirit of God does not originate from earth, but is a divine gift. It is noteworthy to realize that what man considers as changing, God considers solid and unchanging.

The Lord Jesus spoke of the flesh as the opposite of the spirit, "That which is born of the flesh is flesh; and that which is born of the Spirit is spirit" (John 3:6). The opposite of "spiritual" is "carnal" (*sarkikós* [4559], fleshly), that is, derived from flesh (*sárx* [4561]). When God acts upon man, His Spirit brings permanence and stability into his life. He ceases to be carnal (*sarkikós*) or, as Paul describes such a man in 1 Corinthians 2:14, *psuchikós* (5591), psychic, directed only by his soul. When the Spirit of God is received by the spirit of man, he changes constitutionally. He becomes a child of God (John 1:12), a spiritual person characterized by the stability that characterizes God. The Apostle Paul would call this established state *katástasis,* establishment, from which comes the word *akatastasía* (181) in 1 Corinthians 14:33 translated "confusion" in the statement that "God is not a god of confusion." There is a settledness and fixed condition about God (*katástasis*). Paul is arguing that the product of God's Spirit is not a changeable character, but solid and, therefore, dependable. This is because His Spirit is the unseen person directing us. The Corinthians, however, were natural or carnal (*psuchikoi* or *sarkikoi*) and therefore not governed by the steadying influence of the Spirit of God.

"Or Came Out the Word of God From You?"

In evident aversion, the Apostle Paul asks two questions of the proud Corinthians to which the expected answers are negative. The first one is, "Or came out the Word of God from you?" This is the first time in the Corinthian epistles that the phrase "the Word of God" occurs. We will do well to determine the meaning of this important phrase. In Greek there are four words with which the sounds of the mouth can be expressed. They are all nouns which come from four different verbs.

The first noun is *phḗmē* (5345), report, from the verb *phēmí* (5436), to speak, to say. From it, we have the compound noun *prophēteía* (4394), prophecy; and the compound verb *prophēteúō* (4395), to prophesy, to speak ahead or forth which is the meaning of the prefix *pró* (4253). Prophesying is speaking forth something beforehand. The second noun is *rhḗma* (4487), saying, which comes from the verb *rhéō* (4483), to speak. And third is the noun *laliá* (2981), speech. This comes from the verb *laléō* (2980), to speak. Fourth is the noun *lógos* (3056), word, from the verb *légō* (3004), to put words in an order, to speak. *Lógos* is what the preincarnate Christ as Spirit is called by John in John 1:1 where we read, "In the beginning was the Word [*Lógos*, intelligence and the expression of that intelligence]." That this expression refers to Christ in His eternal coexistence with the Father, there is no doubt (John 1:1, 18). This eternal intelligence which gave birth to everything (John 1:3, 4) became flesh, man (John 1:14), so that He could express to us in a manner we could understand that God is Spirit (John 4:24) and that, as such, He came to indwell us (John 1:14). The Word of God then is the eternal Christ who became God's expression to man and the indwelling possession of the believer.

The phrase translated "of God" in Greek is actually "of the God" which means of the Father (John 1:1). Jesus Christ, in His incarnation, did not hide that He was sent by the Father as we find in John 4:34, "My meat is to do the will of Him who sent Me and to finish His work" (see also John 5:30, 37; 6:38–39, 44; 7:16, 18, 28, 33, etc.). Therefore, the Word of God means Christ: His incarnation, His crucifixion, His resurrection, and His message to the world as revealed in the written record of His life and teaching.

GOD'S WORD IS SETTLED AND UNCHANGEABLE

There are two verbs which are used here in verse 36. The first is the verb *exélthen*, the third person singular aorist active indicative of *exérchomai* (1831), to come out, referring to the Word of God in the question. The Corinthians were so proud that one would think that God had chosen them to bestow His revelation or to reveal Himself through His Son. The expected answer is No, of course the Word of God did not come out first from Corinth. The Corinthians were not the original proclaimers of it nor was it among them that Jesus Christ was born and taught and was crucified and raised Himself from the dead.

"Or Came It Unto You Only?"

The second verb used is *katéntēsen,* the third person singular aorist active indicative of *kantantáō* (2658), to settle down. It is found in the question, "Or did it [the Word of God] finally settle down only with you?" The verb *katantáō* is a compound verb derived from *katá* (2596) used as an intensive or meaning "down to" and the verb *antáō* which is not found in the New Testament in this basic form, meaning "to meet with" as if coming from the opposite end. It indicates a stopping point, a settling, and it stands in contrast to *exérchomai,* to come out of. Paul wanted the Corinthians to realize that they were not the originators of the Word of God nor the ones upon whom it finally settled. The one verb "came out of" (*exélthen*) indicates origination, whereas this verb "settled down" (*katéntēsen*) indicates the ultimate goal. We could indicate the meaning of the last question as, Or with you alone has the Word of God settled or found its realization?

Paul thus reproaches the Corinthian church by telling them that they are not the only church in which the Word of God found its beginning and its end as the body of Christ. In 1 Corinthians 4:6 Paul uses the verb *phusióō* (5448), to puff up, from the verb *phusáō,* (n.f. in NT) to blow or inflate, to indicate the pride of the Corinthian church. They had an inflated idea about themselves thinking that they were the only ones from whom the Word of God came forth and the only ones (*mónous*, the accusative plural masculine adjective of *mónos* [3441], only one) on whom finally it rested. In verses 18 and 19 he writes, "Now some are puffed up, as though I would not come to you. But I will come to you shortly, if the Lord will, and will know not the speech of them which are puffed up, but the power." They were not only proud, but they liked to talk about it. In 1 Corinthians 5:2 Paul writes, "And you are puffed up, and have not rather mourned, that he that has done this deed might be taken away from among you." This refers to a man from among their number who had committed incest. He recognized that there were people who had knowledge, but he told them in 1 Corinthians 8:1 that knowledge "puffs up." And, finally, in the great hymn of love in his letter to them in 1 Corinthians 13:4, Paul does not hesitate to tell them that this puffing up is a sign that they lacked that divine love which brings a modest and humble attitude to a person.

LESSONS:

1. Paul states that the Corinthian church was different than all the other churches (v. 33).
2. It was the only church which was characterized by noise and turbulence to the point that outsiders coming into their worship service would think they were maniacs (v. 23).
3. God, however, was not the author of confusion but of order. Therefore, they demonstrated that they followed after a different worship.
4. Paul asked the Corinthians two questions: Did the Word of God originate with them; did it settle down with them? The answer to both questions was negative.
5. The indwelling Spirit of God brings about a quiet and modest behavior in the child of God.

GOD'S WORD IS SETTLED AND UNCHANGEABLE

1 Cor. 14:37

Commandments of the Lord

If any man think himself to be a prophet, or spiritual, let him acknowledge that these things which I write unto you are the commandments of the Lord.

From verse 37 to verse 40 Paul gives his final conclusion of the entire subject of the commotion that existed in the Corinthian church because they spoke in an unknown tongue or in languages that were not interpreted, and more than one spoke at a time, thus making a great deal of noise and confusion.

"If Any Man Think Himself to Be a Prophet, or Spiritual"

This verse begins with the hypothetical conjunction "if" (*ei* [1487]), providing a subjective supposition which is separate from real experience: "If one [*tis* {5100}, the nominative singular masculine indefinite pronoun meaning a certain one or someone] thinks himself [*dokeí*, the third person singular present active indicative of *dokéō* {1380}, to think] to be [*eínai* {1511}, the present infinitive of *eimí* {1510}, to be] a prophet [*prophētēs* {4396}, derived from the preposition *pró* {4253} which means either before or forth, and *phēmí* {5346}, to tell, to speak]."

A prophet was a person who received a message from God and told it to the people, or he was one to whom the future was revealed and he would tell that which was to take place before it happened. The gift of prophecy, in verse 3, was that which brought edification, exhortation, and comfort. This could be given only in a language that was understood by others who heard it. In 1 Corinthians 14:1 Paul begins this whole subject of church worship by telling the Corinthians, "But pursue this love [*tḗn* {3588}, the {which is the accusative singular feminine article of *ho*}; *agápēn*, the accusative of *agápē* {26}, referring to the divine love described in ch. 13] and be zealous rather concerning spiritual things, but more so that you may prophesy."

The person who thought himself to be spiritual (*pneumatikós* [4152]) and directed by the Spirit of God stands in antithesis to the carnal person [*sarkikós* {4559}, obsessed and directed by his *sárx* {4561}, flesh, or *psuchikós* {5591}, soul]. Such a carnal person is directed by his flesh or soul as are the animals (1 Cor. 2:10–15; 3:1–4).

"Let Him Acknowledge"

"Let him acknowledge" is *epiginōskétō*, the third person singular present active imperative of *epiginṓskō* (1921), to fully know experientially. This compound verb is derived from the preposition *epí* (1909), upon, denoting concentration or fullness, and *ginṓskō* (1097), to know experientially. It stands in contrast to the verb *oída*, the perfect used as the present of *eídō* (1492), to know intuitively, to realize. Usually, the translators fail to differentiate between the two words *ginṓskō* and *eídō* or *oída*. Consequently, this has contributed to much confusion in the understanding of the New Testament.

"That These Things That I Write Unto You"

Here the command of the Apostle Paul is that each time we read what he writes, if we consider ourselves prophets or spiritual people, we must know that his messages are written as an apostle of Jesus Christ and not as an ordinary Christian. This is why in

1 Corinthians 9:1 Paul stresses his apostolicity and that what he writes ought to be taken as having been spoken by an apostle of Jesus Christ. The verb being in the present imperative implies that it ought not to be examined lightly, but as pertaining to one's own experience in life.

What is Paul referring to by the expression, "These things that I write unto you"? Generally, he means all the things that he wrote to the Corinthians, and in particular the contents of chapters 11 to 14 of his first epistle that have to do with the order of the church service in Corinth. Observe that he says, "These things [*há*, the accusative plural neuter relative pronoun of *hós* {3739}], which I write [*gráphō* {1125}, I write, the present indicative]."

"Are the Commandments of the Lord"

What Paul wrote did not constitute cultural precepts (*entálmata* [1778], religious injunctions which found their establishment in culture or in individual people and not God). That which comes from God is called *entolē* (1785), a commandment from God. See Matthew 15:9; Mark 7:7; Colossians 2:22 where, regretfully, in the King James Version and the New American Standard Version the word *entálmata* is translated as "commandments." In other translations it is rendered as "human teachings" (Living Bible); "man-made rules" (Today's English Version); "human precepts" (RSV), and "human commands" (NIV). What Paul prescribed for us to follow are not human precepts or cultural admonitions, but divine commandments of the Lord given to him as God's inspired apostle. Unfortunately, if we do not like the Lord's commandments, we tend to say that they are the opinions of Paul and not of the Lord. Paul counteracts this contention in this verse.

In relation to this, one of the big issues in 1 Corinthians 11 through 14 is God's creation of man and woman. Both were created equal before God (Gal. 3:28), and both men and women have free access to God and are fellow heirs of the grace of God (1 Pet. 3:7). But at the same time, Paul wants us to realize that they were created differently, although they were both created in the image of God (Gen. 1:27), that is, with God's Spirit indwelling them. They were created physically different from each other although their differences are not such as to preclude them from being of the same genus (Gen. 2:21–25). God established marriage and made it a mysterious union having one head. Ungodly men, however, have elected not to respect the principle that God has established that the husband should love his wife as himself and not order her about; and in his godly and selfless love, she is to find her submission. If there is no respect for this law of God regarding the function of the human race, the consequences of disobedience will follow. In our society today, we have failed to acknowledge that our sorry state of affairs is a direct result of our disobedience to God. We have thrown away the Lord's instructions for a true and harmonious union of human beings and have reverted to an animal-like state. The only way to return to the blessedness that creation and redemption meant to impart to us is to go back to God's pattern which is one male and one female united in holy matrimony.

LESSONS:

1. A prophet is a spiritual person directed by the Spirit of God. Note the comparative particle *é* (2228), or: "If any man thinks himself to be a prophet or spiritual." In Paul's view, one cannot be a prophet of God and not be spiritual, indwelt by God's Spirit.
2. Paul does not use the basic verb *ginōskétō* (1097), let him know, but the compound *epiginōskétō* (1921) which means to know fully and experientially. It is tantamount with "let him believe" the things that I write that they are the Lord's commandments.
3. There is a difference between *entolaí* (1785), commandments, and *entálmata* (1778), human precepts (Matt. 15:1–9; Col. 2:22).

1 Cor. 14:38

You Cannot Ignore God's Commandments

But if any man is ignorant, let him be ignorant.

Paul stresses the fact that he is an apostle and that he does not speak his own opinions. What he has written is to be taken seriously as the commandments of God. Of course, Paul recognizes that man is a free human being and that he can choose to accept or reject his message as authoritative from the Lord.

"But if Any Man Be Ignorant"

Again, this verse begins with the suppositional subjective conjunction *ei* (1487), if. The verb *agnoeí*, ignores, is in the third person singular present active indicative of *agnoéō* (50), to ignore. It is derived from the privative alpha or a (1), not, and *noéō* (3539), to understand. This refers to voluntary ignorance *(ágnoia* [52]) which is the result of unbelief and will bear its consequences.

The idea is that we should not place the responsibility of our present calamities on being God's choice for us. He did not capriciously choose to punish us. He placed before us a choice which is a concomitant of freedom. None of us would prefer slavery to freedom. God created us in His own image which involved freedom to choose. He placed before us two different ways and told us where these two roads would lead—the one to heaven and the other to hell. Mankind thought he knew better, and we, as human beings, acted through our representatives of the human race, Adam and his wife, Eve. We deceived ourselves by assuming to know a better way and where it would lead us. It appeared prosperous and promising, but it was deceiving and has led us to ruin. We did not exercise trust in God's specific command (Gen. 2:16, 17; 3:1–3).

God did not want to deprive us of what He designed for our sustenance, but as our creator, He wanted us to realize that we could not foretell what would be the result of our choice. He pointed out the fruit of the tree that man was to refrain from eating. The trouble came when Adam and Eve thought the gift of decision making and arriving at their own conclusion was a safe compass. They could not imagine that God knew more than they did. It is like a mother telling her young child not to do so and so, without explaining why. She does not explain because she knows that the child's mind is not capable of comprehending the outcome. It is the result of obedience or disobedience that is her concern.

The verb *noéō* (3539), to perceive, understand, or know, is related to the word *noús* (3563), mind. The gift of the mind is God's gift to the human race which enables a person to think. It derives from the verb *ginṓskō* (1097), to experientially know. The *noús*, or mind, of the New Testament is expressed in the Old Testament Septuagint by the noun *kardía* (2588), heart. The human mind is not enough to make a human being change the direction of his life from evil to saintly. To comprehend with the mind is not enough to save anybody. To believe is absolutely essential. Paul says in Romans 10:9 "That if you will confess with your mouth the Lord Jesus and will believe in your heart that God has raised Him from the dead, you will be saved."

Whereas the Old Testament uses the word "heart" to denote the spiritual, intellectual, emotional, rational, and volitional inner man, the New Testament expresses each faculty separately, especially the cognitive part, the *noús,* and the believing or surrendering of the will, the human spirit, to the Divine Spirit as a heart process. When thinking is influenced by God's Spirit, it becomes belief or faith which changes a person from a sinful being to a spiritual, new creation (2 Cor. 5:17). When the heart is converted, the mind is also changed. However, this changed mind needs to be constantly conformed to the mind of Christ. In Romans 12:2 Paul says, "Be not conformed to this world: but be you transformed by the renewing of your mind, that you may prove what is that good, and acceptable, and perfect will of God."

The word *noús* (mind) occurs several times in 1 Corinthians and always in an endeavor to conform our minds to the mind of Christ. In 1 Corinthians 1:10 Paul says, "Now I beseech you, brethren, by the name of our Lord Jesus Christ, that you all speak [*légēte* {3004}] the same thing, and that there be no divisions among you; but that you be perfectly joined together in the same mind and in the same judgment."

The Corinthian believers were indeed believers in spite of the fact that they were divided into parties (1 Cor. 1:11–17). Their minds needed to conform to the mind of Christ. In 1 Corinthians 2:16 Paul asks, "For who has known the mind of the Lord, that he may instruct Him?" He asserts that knowing the mind (*noús*) of Christ for an individual believer is a matter of constant pursuit, but one which never can be fully recognized. Nevertheless, let us be comforted that we can have the mind of Christ because we can study what He said and did as an expression of His eternity as Christ.

In 1 Corinthians 14:14, 15 (twice), 19, the word *noús* (mind) occurs four times. In all four instances it has to do with the Corinthian phenomenon of speaking in an unknown tongue.

In 1 Corinthians 14:14 Paul says, "For if I pray in an unknown tongue, my spirit prays, but my understanding [*noús*] is unfruitful." Here Paul draws the distinction between the spirit of the believer and his mind. They are two different things. His spirit is already under the influence of the Spirit of God. It is regenerated. But his mind needs to be developed. It needs to bear the fruit of the Spirit spoken of in Galatians 5:22, 23. For this conformity of our spirit to the Holy Spirit, we need to exercise God's wonderful gift to us, His mind, in the process of development. My spirit under the influence of the Spirit of God never annuls the mind which He gave me.

In 1 Corinthians 14:15 Paul asserts that the believer may claim he does one thing with his spirit and not with his enlightened mind. The two are spoken of as one faculty, both in the Old and New Testament as "heart" meaning man's spirit and man's mind. But the two are activated by the same Spirit and one does not act independently of the other. "What is it then? I will pray with the spirit [my spirit], and I will pray with the understanding [*noús,* mind] also: I will sing with the spirit [my spirit], and I will sing with the understanding [*noús*] also." The two, the spirit and the mind, function together. They are separately distinguished, but they have the same controller, the Spirit of God. The one cannot be actively directed one way and the other in another direction.

In 1 Corinthians 14:19 Paul recognized that, in a sane person like himself, his spirit was always directed by his mind. He writes: "Yet in the church I had rather speak five words with my understanding [*noús,* mind], that by my voice I might teach others also, than ten thousand words in an unknown tongue."

Then in 1 Corinthians 14:37 Paul uses the verb *epiginōskétō,* let him fully experientially know, the third singular present active imperative of *epiginōskō* (1921), to fully experientially know. "If [the subjective suppositional conjunction] any man think himself to be a prophet or a spiritual person [even though he may not be], let him fully experientially know [*epiginōskétō*] that the things that I write unto you are the commandments [*entolaí*

{1785}, commandments as contrasted to *entálmata* {1778}, traditional precepts] of the Lord."

Paul has been telling the Corinthians how to behave in the church gatherings. Do not speak without activating the mind. When speaking, say something that edifies the church. In order that they may be edified, they must understand what is said. God never spoke in any language but the language of the people. When He announced the coming of His Son, He spoke through an angel to the virgin Mary (Luke 1:28–38) and to the Jewish shepherds in Hebrew, a language that she and they all understood (Luke 2:10–14). To the Chaldeans in Babylon, He spoke through the language of the stars since they understood astronomy. When He spoke to the fish that swallowed Jonah, He spoke so the fish could understand. Comprehension was His concern, and it ought to be ours.

"Let Him Be Ignorant"

This phrase is translated from *agnoeítō*, the third person singular present active imperative of *agoéō*, ignore, which is the reading of the Textus Receptus and the Majority Text which we adopt. It means that a man is free to ignore these truths, but he is not free to choose the consequences of his ignorance. To ignore means not to allow something to occupy the mind. The United Bible Society text, which some translations prefer, has the verb *agnoeítai*, the third person singular present passive indicative which means "he is ignored." Paul does not lay the threat of being ignored on the Lord, but he rather attributes the ignorance that plagues the human race as a natural consequence of man's choice.

Paul says that if anybody wants to follow a different course than God has prescribed, he must accept the responsibility of his own action. If he acts in a disorderly manner in the church, he appears to the world as a maniac (1 Cor. 14:23). The evil he brings upon the name of God is incalculable. He gives the impression that God is the author of confusion (v. 33). Is our manner of worship giving the world the wrong impression of our God?

LESSONS:

1. Agnosticism is related to the Greek verb *agnoéō* (50), to be ignorant.
2. To be an agnostic is to declare that one is ignorant.
3. One who chooses to be ignorant must assume the responsibility of ignorance and not attempt to convey the idea that there is not enough evidence of the truth of God to convince him. Jesus said, "I am the way and the truth and the life. Nobody comes to the Father but by me" (John 14:6).
4. What Paul wrote to the Corinthians about decent and orderly Christian worship ought to be taken seriously as a command of the Lord (v. 37).

1 Cor. 14:39

Be Zealous in Prophesying

Wherefore, brethren, be zealous in prophesying, and forbid not to speak with tongues.

The passage of 1 Corinthians 14:12–14 reveals Paul's attitude and philosophy of prophesying:

> Even so you, forasmuch as you are zealous [*zēlōtaí*, the plural of *zēlōtḗs* {2207}, zealot; the verb *zēloúte* {2206}, be zealous, used in v. 39] of spiritual gifts, seek that you may excel to the edifying of the church. Wherefore let him who speaks in an unknown tongue [note it is singular] pray that he may interpret. For if I pray in an unknown tongue [singular], my spirit prays, but my understanding is unfruitful.

Paul has categorically stressed the importance of the clarity of one's speech for the sake of the others as he writes to the Corinthians.

"Wherefore, Brethren"

Paul's loving spirit prevails throughout his letters. Although he does not agree with the Corinthians in their practice of speaking in an unknown tongue, he does not brand them as heretics. He calls them his brethren. Would that this spirit prevailed in Christian churches today. We ought always to speak the truth in love and never reject fellow believers because of differences of interpretation of Scripture or practice where it does not involve the fundamentals of the faith. Let us emulate Paul and call them "brethren."

"Be Zealous in Prophesying"

The Greek word for "be zealous" is *zēloûte*, to eagerly desire. It is the same word Paul used at the outset of this chapter and it comes from the Greek substantive *zêlos* (2205), meaning zeal. Seek with zeal, pursue actively, is Paul's command. This is not coveting in the sense of desiring the possessions of another. We as Christians should not seek things or virtues simply because others have them, but because of their intrinsic value as revealed by God Himself in His Word. Once we are convinced that something is God's will for us, however, we should seek it with zeal. This zeal is lacking in the pulpit and the pew today.

The emotional ecstasies of the Corinthians were indeed an evidence of zeal. It is obvious from the whole tenor of 1 Corinthians 14 that their practice of speaking in an unknown tongue was a noisy, disorderly, confusing exhibition of misdirected zeal. That is why Paul admonishes them in verse 33 that "God is not the author of confusion, but of peace."

The verb *zēloûte* (2206) is in the present imperative, which would indicate continuous action. The Corinthians were to continuously and earnestly seek to prophesy. Paul urges them to put all their zeal into telling forth the grace and revelation of God.

"And Forbid Not to Speak With Tongues"

Observe that the command to prophesy is connected with the command, "And forbid not to speak with tongues." It is not connected by the adversative "but," but by the connective "and" (*kai* [2532]). "Tongues" here does not stand in contrast to prophesying but is regarded as a means of accomplishing it. To prophesy, one must make the counsel of God clear to his or her listeners. Unknown tongues cannot accomplish this. We have seen throughout our study on 1 Corinthians 14 that Paul has used the singular form, "a tongue," with a singular subject, to refer to unknown ecstatic utterances as in verses 2, 4, 13, 19, 26, 27 and the plural form, "tongues," with a singular subject to refer to known, understandable languages as in verses 5, 6, 18, 22. Tongues, or understandable foreign languages, are consistent with the use of prophecy and are to be permitted. Such would not be the case if Paul were merely tolerating tongue-speaking as opposed to prophecy. In the latter case, he would have said, Be zealous to prophesy, but forbid not to speak with a tongue if an interpreter is present. But in this verse he makes no mention of an interpreter which would seem to rule out ecstatic utterances. Why would Paul say, Forbid not to speak in ecstatic utterances such as would lead unbelievers to think you are a madman when you practice them in public?

Paul's meaning here can best be understood by a concrete illustration. Suppose, as sometimes happens, that an English speaking preacher should be visiting Greece. Should he be forbidden to speak in English to the Greek brethren in their worship services? Not as long as he can be understood, either directly or through an interpreter. Naturally, it would be inconceivable for him to address them in English if no one understood him and there was no interpreter present. Even human languages can cause disorder in a congregation if they cannot be understood. The principle of understandability applies to speaking in an unknown tongue as well as to speaking in foreign languages.

We normally speak in our own native language to those who speak and understand it as we do. When necessary to accomplish the purpose of prophesying, we may speak in a foreign language, either by the direct enablement of God or through having learned it naturally. Paul's whole thesis in this discussion of speaking in the public worship service is that whatever is said, whether in human languages or an unknown tongue, must be understandable, either directly or through an interpreter, if it is to edify the congregation. When telling the Corinthians not to forbid speaking in tongues, Paul must mean what he has already argued as being acceptable in the public worship service. The word "tongues" is all-inclusive, with the very basic assumption that these tongues are understood, whether they be an unknown tongue through an interpreter or any human language, the latter either directly understood by the hearers or interpreted through a translator.

Paul may also have been concerned lest the Corinthians go to the other extreme and forbid speaking in foreign languages altogether which, of course, are deemed acceptable if they are interpreted.

LESSONS:

1. Though the Apostle Paul did not endorse their glossolalia, he refused to disassociate himself from them. He called them "brethren." Jesus had a similar policy (Luke 9:49, 50).
2. It is possible to have a fervent zeal but one that is uninformed. See Romans 10:2.
3. Our zeal to speak and teach the Word of God should be paramount in our lives.
4. It is foolish to speak in a tongue or tongues when no one can understand.
5. Speakers of foreign languages should have an interpreter.

1 Cor. 14:40

Decorum in the House of God

Let all things be done decently and in order.

Corinth was a city where people from different cultures lived and spoke many languages. One of the questions that the Apostle Paul pointedly addressed to the Corinthians was that which he asks in 1 Corinthian 4:7, "For who makes you to differ from another?" The variety of cultures and means of communication are attributable to God Himself, for He has built variety into His creation. There is no better illustration found anywhere than that of the members of the human body which Paul speaks about in 1 Corinthians 12:12–26. That which makes us alike as human beings and that which makes us different are all ascribed to God, the Creator. So also, by God's will, human beings were created male and female. All people are equal, but different. And the sooner that we acknowledge our equality as God-given, the sooner we shall acknowledge our differences also as God-given and shall be eager to discover our particular functions within our differences. Paul continues in 1 Corinthians 4:7: "And what have you that you did not receive?" Let us each acknowledge that what we are and what we have come from God, and that it is according to His predetermination, and that He makes no mistakes. Paul then asks, in the balance of this verse, "Now if you did receive it, why do you glory as if you had not received it?" Our differences should cause us to consider ourselves neither superior nor inferior to others.

Chapter 12 of 1 Corinthians speaks of spiritual gifts, and then in chapter 13, Paul breaks forth in his hymn of love. This is followed by chapter 14 which we are studying and which speaks of prophesying and the means whereby this can be done, that is, through speech, using the God-given instrument of the tongue. In this chapter, Paul elaborates on the gift of prophecy and the gift of tongues.

There is, however, a complete misunderstanding as to who may use these gifts of God. Men only, or also women? If a woman was to keep absolutely silent in the church service, she would be instructed not to prophesy and not to pray or sing. However, in 1 Corinthians 11:5 women did pray and prophesy, and 1 Corinthians 14:26 refers to every one of them singing or "a psalm." All involved speech, of course, but, according to Paul, the women should not do it with their heads uncovered or with their hair not distinctively showing that they are women. Their heads could be covered by either a veil or their naturally long hair (1 Cor. 11:5, 6).

In Corinth, a phenomenon had occurred in public worship which was the ecstatic speaking in an unknown tongue. It is evident, as one reads 1 Corinthians 14, that this resulted in a noisy worship service. Paul did not want the husbands to permit or encourage their wives to increase the noise that was so prevalent during the Corinthian worship. As we read this chapter, we must differentiate between the ecstatic speaking in an unknown tongue and speaking in languages other than the one understood by the listeners. Comprehension of what was said made prophesying meaningful. The important thing in any Christian worship is the edification of those who are present. When one speaks in a foreign language or in an unknown tongue and it is not interpreted, then others do not understand and cannot say "Amen" (v. 16).

In our careful study of the fourteenth chapter, we have discovered that when "tongue" is used in the singular, as in verses 2 and 4, with a singular subject, reference is made to speaking in an unknown tongue. The King James Version has rightly expressed it as an "unknown tongue." However, when Paul uses the plural noun "tongues," he refers to ethnic languages known to the speaker but unknown to the listeners.

In verse 5, Paul says, "I desire that you all spoke with tongues [languages]." He further adds, "But rather that you prophesied, for greater is he that prophesies than he that speaks with tongues [languages] except he interpret, that the church may receive edifying." Prophesying requires a comprehension of what is being said.

Now Paul was a polyglot, but not a glossolaliac. He spoke a variety of languages, certainly Hebrew, Greek, and Latin but he would not dream of speaking in one of those languages if his audience could not understand it. In verse 6 he says, "Now brethren, if I come unto you speaking with tongues [languages unknown to you], what shall I profit you?"

And then in verse 9 Paul speaks of the tongue as a member of the human body used as a means of communication. However, one is to use it to form meaningful and intelligible words (eúsēmon [2154], meaningful; lógon [3056], intelligible word) and not incomprehensible sounds.

After definitely saying that what comes from the human tongue should be the result of a man's intelligence, Paul speaks of his own knowledge of languages in verse 18: "I thank my God, I speak with tongues [languages] more than you all." Paul cannot speak here of the unknown ecstatic tongue of the Corinthians, for he would not pride himself for what he condemns them for doing. Then in verse 19 he says, "Yet in the church I had rather speak five words with my understanding, that by my voice I might teach others also, than ten thousand words in an unknown tongue [singular]."

It is in this context that Paul's prohibition of the speaking of the women [wives] should be interpreted. When he says in verse 34 that it is forbidden for the women [wives] to speak, he means to speak or behave in such a way that God's order of worship should be violated, for God is a God of order and peace, not disorder. It is noteworthy that Paul closes this chapter with the clear admonition—

"Let All Things Be Done Decently"

Here Paul gives his final injunction concerning speaking with tongues. "Let all things be done decently and in order" (v. 40). When translating this verse the KJV translators left out the particle *dé* (1161) which the United Bible Society and Nestle's texts have as part of the verse. This particle can best be rendered by implication here as "only." It provides an underlying condition of prophesying in one's own or any other language. "Only" do it decently and in order. In other words, speaking without thought in any language can cause confusion and indecorum. This concerns not only the nature of the language but also the manner of speaking. Remember this, the Apostle says: Whatever you say and in no matter what language you say it, "let all things be done only decently and in order."

The word "decently" translates the Greek adverb *euschēmónōs* (2156) which in Romans 13:13 and 1 Thessalonians 4:12 is translated in the King James Version as "honestly." The word is derived from *eu* (2095), well or good, and *schēma* (4976), external form, appearance. The adverb, therefore, means that a spiritual person is not only transformed inwardly by the Spirit of God, but also outwardly in his external behavior thus demonstrating a stable character. Apparently the stability that characterized God was lacking in the Corinthian behavior in worship.

"Ecclesiastical decorum" is what is meant here. "Beauty and harmony prevail in God's universe, where each part discharges its proper function without slackness or encroachment; and beauty and harmony ought to prevail in the worship of God." (Plummer and Robertson, *The International Critical Commentary, 1 Corinthians.* Minneapolis, MN: Fortress, 1914:328.)

"And In Order"

In the expression *kaí* (2532) *katá* (2596) *táxin* (5010) (and according to order), translated "and in order," some see a military metaphor. Soldiers must march in order or they will never succeed. The end will be confusion and defeat. The expression as such occurs only here in the New Testament. Herodotus used it to describe the Greek's manner of fighting at Salamis as opposed to the disorderly efforts of the barbarians (Herodotus VIII:86). Each element in Christian worship and in prophesying has its God-ordained order. This speaks of the creative act of God as having followed a pattern and not a haphazard evolvement. He created everything in order to accomplish a specific purpose, the result of which is peace. When there is lack of order, God Himself is absent from the proceedings, for it is He who has created an orderly universe and man himself, whose body and mind work with such harmony, system, and order as to defy human imagination. How could a similar order possibly be lacking in His new spiritual creation in and through Christ?

Thus in 1 Corinthians 12—14, the Apostle Paul has indicated the dangers of spiritual anarchy. When each Christian regards himself as having a special gift implanted by the Holy Spirit, and each is allowed to demonstrate it at will in public worship, utter confusion results. This disrupts the congregation, dismays those who want to worship "decently and in order," repels unbelievers, and reflects negatively on the character of God Himself.

In our interpretation of this portion of Scripture and the total question of "tongues," we have endeavored to be honest and logical. First Corinthians 14 has perplexed the best of commentators because Paul seems to be arguing both for and against the same thing. If this is so, it constitutes an insurmountable problem.

We do not believe it to be so, for he could not be for and against the same thing. This is the basic logical assumption on which we take our stand. As we have proceeded to examine the text in the greatest possible detail, we have been persuaded that what we have presented constitutes the most logical conclusion.

One must not take any one argument or any one verse in isolation, but consider the whole thrust of Paul's arguments and try to relate them to the basic conclusions regarding the historic instances of speaking in tongues in Scripture. This we have done. Our discussion on some points may seem debatable or inconclusive taken in isolation, but so do the points themselves as they stand in Scripture if taken alone without the buttressing arguments of the whole context. However, we believe that the cumulative weight of the arguments we have presented in this study is difficult to disregard. Any interpretation of any isolated statement must have inherently the same measure of weakness as the statement itself standing on its own without being related to the total argument of the whole context and the basic assumptions derived from the general thesis. Therefore, any statement made by the Apostle Paul, isolated from 1 Corinthians chapter fourteen, can have no absolute meaning.

Take verse 18, for instance. "I thank my God I speak with tongues more than you all." What kind of tongues does Paul mean? Taken in isolation, this verse can lead to no conclusion; but if we take the total argument we realize that these tongues must have the following qualities:

(1) They must be understandable by the hearers, either directly or through an interpreter.

(2) The speaker must know what he is saying.

(3) They must result in edification.

Having determined these basic conclusions derived from the general thesis of the chapter, we can logically conclude that these tongues must be understandable human languages. But we cannot conclude this from this one verse alone.

Consider verse 23 also as an illustration. Here Paul says that non-experts in spiritual things, coming into a Christian assembly and hearing the Corinthians collectively speaking in tongues, will conclude that they are insane. Here the plural "tongues" is used with the plural subject "all." It refers collectively to each one of the Corinthians speaking in an unknown tongue. What tongues are these? Again if we take this verse just by itself we can hardly arrive at the proper conclusion. Could it be that Paul is speaking here of the same tongues that he said he himself spoke and that he wished everyone else spoke? The assumption is that this is impossible. Otherwise, he would be contradicting himself. Therefore, we must arrive at the conclusion, again from the general discussion of the theme, that these must be tongues that neither the speaker nor the hearers understand and that do not edify. Therefore, our assumption that we have two kinds of tongues is on a solid basis that is almost impossible to refute. Let us call each other "brethren" and not vilify or reject one another because of differences in practice. For though we speak with the tongues of men and of angels and have not love, we might as well not call ourselves Christians at all.

One last word of advice. Do not judge the Word of God from any experience you may have had. It is the other way around. The reality and genuineness of experience must be judged from the Word of God. If our own experiences become the criterion, the Bible ceases to be our absolute authority!

LESSONS:

1. Judging from the *kósmos* (2889), our Creator is organized. He is pleased when those who worship Him in spirit and in truth (John 4:23, 24) do so in an orderly manner.
2. God has built variety into His creation. However, it is orderly and each variety was created for a specific purpose.
3. God is a God of peace, and where there is no order, there is no peace.
4. Our behavior, especially in God's house, reflects our Lord Himself. How do you represent your Lord?
5. The final authority for anything and everything is the Word of God. It alone is worthy of our absolute trust.

Scripture Index